Sound Discovery®

A Synthetic Phonics Programme for the Teaching of Reading, Spelling and Writing. Suitable for First-Time, Slow-to-Start and Dyslexic Learners of all ages, including adults.

A handbook of words and sentences for reading and dictation
Steps 4 to 7

Dr Marlynne Grant
Educational Psychologist

RIDGEHILL PUBLISHING

First Published September 2001

Ridgehill Publishing,
32 Ridgehill,
Henleaze,
Bristol,
BS9 4SB.

Tel: (+44 or 0) 117 962 2670
Fax: (+44 or 0) 117 962 8344
www.ridgehillpublishing.com

"Arial" typeface was selected for the relevant teaching sections rather than "Sassoon Infant" because students who are extending their literacy skills are more likely to encounter the former in everyday life.

ISBN 1 84556 064 7

About the Author

Marlynne Grant
BSc, CertEd, MEdPsych, PhD, AFBPsS, CPsychol

The author is an Educational Psychologist who works part-time for a
Local Educational Authority. She also works as an Independent
Educational Psychologist specialising in specific learning difficulties/ dyslexia
and literacy difficulties. She has written other resource materials
for literacy development. This book has been written from her work and
experience over twenty years with students and teachers.

Acknowledgements

My special thanks to Trudy Wainwright, Special Educational Needs Co-
ordinator and Special Needs Teacher whose inspiration, ideas, encouragement
and support have been invaluable in the preparation of this book. Grateful
thanks also to Sheila Leech and Joanna Lunt, Educational Psychologists, to
Headteacher and other staff at St Michael's School, Stoke Gifford, Liz Lang,
Head of the Language and Communication Resource Base at Filton High
School and to Sue Hunt, SENCO at King Edmund's Secondary School. I very
much appreciate that these colleagues, along with others, have been generous
with their time and willingness to discuss the ideas and materials in this book
and to offer their suggestions.

Contents

pages

Sound Discovery® is based on sounds. It can be used for first-time teaching or as an intervention programme for literacy difficulties. It is suitable for all ages from infant to adult and can provide stable and *sound* literacy learning and recovery.

Sound Discovery® was especially written to prevent literacy difficulties occurring at the outset with beginners and also to effect change when difficulties are experienced.

Sound Discovery® was developed to be used by teachers who wish to give their young pupils the very best start and then to extend this learning. It is also suitable for those students whose poor literacy impairs their access to the curriculum. It will be an invaluable resource for teachers who encounter dyslexia in their students.

Sound Discovery® teaches through a careful sequence of steps which progress from simple to complex. **Synthetic phonics** is at the heart of *Sound Discovery*® making it an effective synthetic phonics programme.

This book provides words and sentences to support the *Sound Discovery*® programme through direct reading and spelling practice.

Research reveals that students with literacy difficulties share a common problem: they have failed to *discover* the alphabetic principle of how the English writing system works.

There are **three powerful tools** for successful reading and spelling. Hence the teaching task for students of all ages is to master these three tools and **apply** them to real reading and spelling. The tools need to be taught directly and they should be at the core of any first-time teaching or intervention programme. They should be the primary focus of teaching as they are the **only** activities which matter in terms of subsequent reading and spelling acquisition.

The **three most powerful tools** for literacy are:

1. Knowledge of the **code** which matches all 42 sounds (phonemes) of spoken English to written letter(s) (graphemes).

2. The phonological skill of **blending** - (for reading).

3. The phonological skill of **segmenting** - being able to hear the sounds in words - (for spelling).

Sound Discovery® aims to teach these three essential tools for literacy. It delivers this teaching in compacted individual sessions which are suitable for any age group and for specific learning difficulties/dyslexia. The ***Sound Discovery***® programme calls these **Snappy Lesson**® sessions as the pace is fast moving. *

It is crucial that students have an automatic grasp of the code which matches sounds to letters and it is important to take some time to build up this automaticity. Fluency and mastery in learning at this stage is vital for subsequent reading comprehension and writing composition.

As soon as students begin to learn the code and can link some consonant and vowel sounds to letters they can immediately start ***applying*** and ***using*** this code knowledge to read and spell words containing these sounds. The phonological skill of synthesis (blending) enables them to read words and the phonological skill of segmenting (hearing the sounds in words) enables them to spell words.

* Footnote: See the Introduction of the *Sound Discovery*® *Manual* (pp. 3-4 and 6-10) for a description of the *Snappy Lesson* ® and for its psychological underpinning which makes it so effective as a teaching tool. Also see the following two pages and pages 116-117.

The *Snappy Lesson*®

The *Snappy Lesson*® structure is recommended for each piece of teaching in *Words and Sentences*, Part 2, because the *Snappy Lesson*® incorporates all the essential elements of synthetic phonics. Nothing should be left out. The time spent on each element is left to the teacher's discretion but what is essential is that all elements should be covered. Half the lesson focuses on reading and the other half on spelling, thus reinforcing that reading and spelling are reversible processes.

The following is an example of a *Snappy Lesson*® at Step 7 of the programme, when special suffixes are being introduced. See pages 116-117 for further details.

READING

1. SPECIAL SUFFIXES   **quick review of any special suffixes already taught**

- Teacher shows the suffix cards photocopied from the *Sound Discovery*® *Manual* pp 93-96.
- Students say whole suffix.

2. SPECIAL SUFFIXES   **teach new suffix**

- Teacher uses suffix card from *Sound Discovery*® *Manual* e.g. -tion.
- Students say whole suffix.

3. BLENDING   **oral blending**

- Teacher says whole syllable(s) and special suffix using "robot arms" if necessary,   e.g.sta-tion, vac-a-tion.
- Students blend the separate chunks into the word.

4. WORD CARDS   (from Step 7, *Sound Discovery*® *Words and Sentences, Part 2*)
     sound and say

- Students sound syllables and special suffix chunk, using "robot arms" if necessary, blend the chunks together and say the word.
- Students sound in their heads and say word.

5. WORD LISTS

- Whole group reads lists from *Sound Discovery*® *Words and Sentences, Part2*.
- Teacher asks individual students to read specific words.

6. SENTENCE READING

- Use *Sound Discovery*® *Words and Sentences, Part 2* and controlled texts.

SPELLING

---

7. SPECIAL SUFFIXES   **quick review of any special suffixes already taught**

- Teacher dictates special suffix chunks.
- Students say each chunk slowly as they write the chunk on small white board. Do not allow them to say letter names as they write the special suffix.

---

8. SPECIAL SUFFIXES   **teach new spelling pattern**

- Teacher explains, "This is the new picture of the special ending/suffix for today."
- Teacher says the special ending and shows the new spelling on a card, photocopied from the *Sound Discovery® Manual* pp. 93-96.
- Teacher models letter formation, saying the chunk slowly as he/she writes it. Teacher does not say letter names.
- Teacher says special suffix to the students.
- Students repeat chunk slowly as they write the suffix. They do not say letter names.

---

9. HEARING THE SYLLABLES AND SPECIAL SUFFIXES IN WORDS

- Teacher says word to group, e.g. station.
- Students repeat the word, saying it slowly to identify the syllable(s) and special suffix, by clapping beats or feeling the lowering of the chin.
- Students say syllable, count phonemes of the syllable on fingers of one hand and show fingers.
- Students say whole suffix and identify it with closed fist of other hand, e.g. s-t-a-/tion.
- Teacher says word to individual student, e.g. vacation.
- Student says syllables and special suffix: vac/a/tion. Student repeats first syllable, identifying phonemes on fingers of one hand, and makes the syllable on board with magnetic phoneme cards from *Sound Discovery® Manual*: v-a-c. Student repeats with other syllable(s):a. Student repeats special suffix and places magnetic suffix card <tion> from *Sound Discovery® Manual* to the right of vac and a.
- Student says word.

---

10. SPELLING

- Teacher dictates word from Step 7, e.g. election.
- Students identify syllables and special suffix: e/lec/tion.
- Students tap phoneme(s) for first syllable on white board.
- Students draw phoneme line(s) for first syllable on white board: _
- Students write in letter(s) and say syllable: <u>e</u>
- Leave a space
- Tap, draw phoneme lines and write in letters for second and subsequent syllables:
  <u>e</u> <u>l</u> <u>e</u> <u>c</u>
- Leave a space.
- Draw a special suffix line and write letters in whilst saying the chunk: <u>tion</u>
- Student says word: <u>e</u> <u>l</u> <u>e</u> <u>c</u>   <u>tion</u>
- Teacher models correct response on board.

---

11. SENTENCES

- Teacher dictates sentences using new spelling pattern from controlled text or from Step 7, *Sound Discovery® Words and Sentences, Part 2.*
- Students write sentence and read it back.
- Teacher models correct response on board.

- Incorporate into independent writing through modelling.

The teaching framework of **Sound Discovery®** is developed over seven teaching steps.

Sound Discovery® Words and Sentences Part 1,

provides materials to practise the first three teaching steps.

This book,

Sound Discovery® Words and Sentences Part 2,

continues the programme and provides words and sentences to practise reading and dictation for the teaching Steps 4 to 7:

Step 4	Teach prefixes and suffixes
Step 5	Teach syllable types
Step 6	Teach syllable division
Step 7	Teach special suffixes

Individual Words for Reading and Dictation

Each page will contain graded, regular words to cut out or to read in lists.   An Arial font has been chosen to extend students' learning to the type of print they are most likely to encounter in everyday life. The words are made up of the suffixes, prefixes, root words/stems, syllables and special suffixes learned in each step. The main function of the words is to provide practice for the two essential phonological skills of synthesis (blending) and phoneme segmentation (hearing the sounds in words) in a more complex setting than in Steps 1-3. Blending is still the key skill when reading more complex words and hearing the sounds in words is still the key skill when spelling more complex words.

For **reading** the student identifies syllables or morphological units (meaning units), scans each in a left to right direction, says the sounds which go with each grapheme in the syllable or unit and blends the sounds together.

For **spelling** the teacher dictates the word, the student identifies the syllables or units orally, identifies the sounds within them and then either makes the word from flash cards or writes the word.

The syllables and units can be taught through the *Snappy Lesson*® described in the *Sound Discovery*® *Manual* and supported by materials from the *Sound Discovery*® *Manual* (flash card sheets).

Root words, stems, suffixes and prefixes are morphological units, i.e. they convey meaning.

Individual Sentences for Reading and Dictation

Each page will contain graded sentences made up of words using the syllables or units learned in each step.

For **reading** the student scans each syllable or unit in a left to right direction, says the sounds which go with each grapheme and blends the sounds together.

For **spelling** the teacher dictates the whole sentence, the student identifies the sounds in each word and then writes each word and the whole sentence. Correct punctuation is required with capital letters and full stops.

The sentences can be used for reading and spelling as described in the *Snappy Lesson®* (see pages 3-4 and 116-117 and also the *Sound Discovery® Manual*).

STEP 4   TEACH PREFIXES, ROOT WORDS AND SUFFIXES

General background introduction for teachers

It is possible to make a structural analysis of polysyllabic words into prefix, stem/root word and suffix/ending. Root words/stems, suffixes and prefixes are morphological units, i.e. they convey meaning. About fifty per cent of English words come from Latin, the language of the Romans; ten to twelve per cent come from Anglo-Saxon, the language of England during the early Middle Ages. The words from both of these languages follow similar **accent** patterns. The Latin words are likely to have a prefix, a stem/root word and a suffix/ending.:

- a **prefix** is likely to be a Latin preposition;
- a **stem/root word** can have one or more syllables. It is the most important part of the word, since it furnishes the basic meaning of the word;
- a **suffix/ending** tells the part of speech - what job the word has in the sentence; the suffix also has a meaning which a dictionary will supply.

Note the prefix comes first, then the stem, followed by a suffix:

prefix	stem	suffix
ad	<u>mitt</u>	ing
con	<u>duct</u>	or
re	<u>li</u>	able
pro	<u>ject</u>	or
re	<u>sist</u>	ant
de	<u>fend</u>	ant
sub	<u>tract</u>	ing
pre	<u>tend</u>	ed

Sometimes the word has only a stem/root word and a suffix:

stem	suffix
<u>act</u>	ive
<u>pay</u>	ment
<u>anim</u>	al
<u>miser</u>	able
<u>pict</u>	ure

Sometimes the word may have a prefix and a stem but no suffix:

prefix	stem
sub	mit
ob	ject
ab	sorb
inter	rupt
ne	glect
in	vite
ex	cite
de	clare

In all these words the underlined parts are the stems. It is usual to place the accent on the stem. When there is no prefix, the first part of the word is the stem and will receive the accent.

If there are two syllables in the stem, accent the first syllable e.g. animal, miserable.

Note that nouns and verbs have different accent patterns:

e.g.   produce   (verb)   produce   (noun)

        transport   (verb)   transport   (noun)

It is important that your students understand the difference between dividing words into syllables and into prefix, stem and suffix. You can illustrate this by dividing words in both ways which will highlight this difference:

syllable division	morphological division
con/nec/ting	con nect ing
un/der/stan/ding	under stand ing

It can be very helpful for correct spelling for students to identify the root of the word.
 e.g. know ledge.   The root word "know" can be pronounced from an analysis of its constituent phonemes: kn-ow (<kn> is an alternative spelling of the /n/ sound
<ow> is an alternative spelling of the /oa/ sound).
However, in the abstract noun "knowledge" derived from the root word "know", the spelling of the root remains the same but the pronunciation changes. The letters <ow> in "knowledge" represent the /o/ sound. A good strategy for remembering the spelling is to "say the word as it is spelled": e.g. know ledge (know to rhyme with snow).

Armed with this background understanding, teachers can now start teaching the next *Sound Discovery*™ step, Step 4 which establishes the concept of the root word, then teaches suffixes and prefixes:

Step 4.1   Establish concept of **root word**

Step 4.2   Teach **suffixes**

Step 4.3   Teach **prefixes**

These units can be taught through the *Snappy Lesson*™ using the flash card materials found in the *Sound Discovery*™ *Manual*, pages 71-86. The words and sentences which follow will allow students to apply their skills for reading and spelling.

Step 4.1   Root Words for Reading and Dictation

Root words, also called stems, furnish the basic meaning of a word. Root words can be taught through the *Snappy Lesson*™ teaching format using the flash card materials found in the *Sound Discovery*™ *Manual*, pages 71-80. The flash cards provide examples of root words. Some of these are polysyllables and students may need help to split them into syllables. They may also need help with identifying all the phonemes in these words and syllables.

Syllable and phoneme splits for the root word flash cards

	syllables	phonemes
connect	con/nect	c-o-nn-e-c-t
remark	re/mark	r-e-m-ar-k
predict	pre/dict	p-r-e-d-i-c-t
touch	touch	t-ou-ch
love	love	l-(o-e)-v where <o-e> is alt sp for /u/
approach	ap/proach	a-pp-r-oa-ch
joy	joy	j-oy
infect	in/fect	i-n-f-e-c-t
respect	re/spect	r-e-s-p-e-c-t
break	break	b-r-ea-k
rely	re/ly	r-e-l-y
argue	ar/gue	ar-g-ue
control	con/trol	c-o-n-t-r-o-l
courage	cour/age	c-our-(a-e)-g (e) <our> is alt sp for /er/
access	ac/cess	a-c-c(e)-e-ss
tradition	trad-i-tion	t-r-a-d-i-ti-o-n (t-r-a-d-i-/shun/)
suggest	sug/gest	s-u-gg(e)-e-s-t
profession	pro/fessi/on	p-r-o-f-e-ssi-o-n
		p-r-o-f-e-/shun/
like	like	l-(i-e)-k
comfort	com/fort	c-o-m-f-or-t
avail	av/ail	a-v-ai-l
consider	con/sid/er	c-o-n-s-i-d-er
drink	drink	d-r-l-n(g)-k
excuse	ex/cuse	e-x-c-(u-e)-s
question	ques/tion	qu-e-s-ti-o-n (qu-e-s-/chun/)
enjoy	en/joy	e-n-j-oy
reason	rea/son	r-ea-s-o-n
agree	ag/ree	a-g-r-ee
suit	suit	s-ui-t
value	val/ue	v-a-l-ue
port	port	p-or-t
turn	turn	t-ur-n

It has been necessary to use additional root words or stems to create a good range of example words in Steps 4.2 and 4.3 such as: kind, happy, sad, compute, teach, small, big, home, shape, bag, marry, mile, refer, differ, prefer, confer, admit, way, spell, human, script. It has also been necessary to use stems which provide meaning but which are not whole words such as:-dict-, -fer-, -fect-.

Step 4.1   Sentences with Root Words for Reading and Dictation

These sentences are designed for students who have already learned Steps 1 to 3 of the *Sound Discovery* programme. Students may need help with:

house	<se> is alternative spelling pattern for the /s/ sound,
baby	<a> is alternative spelling pattern for the /ai/ sound,
have, give, gives	<ve> is alternative spelling pattern for the /v/ sound,
were	<ere> is alternative spelling pattern for the /er/ sound,
their	<eir> is alternative spelling pattern for the /air/ sound.

Irregular words are "the", "to", "you", "of" "into".

1. Can you connect the ends of the pipes?

2. That remark was not kind.

3. I predict they will win.

4. Touch my hand!

5. I love you.

6. The approach to the house is a steep hill.

7. A new baby can bring much joy.

8. This bug may infect you

9. The class respect their teacher.

10. Break the ice on the pond.

11. You can rely on me.

12. My sisters argue all the time.

13. He tries to control his temper.

14. The brave men had a lot of courage.

15.   This path gives access to the beach.

16.   It is a tradition to sing the school song.

17.   I suggest you go now.

18.   Her profession is law.

19.   I like his coat.

20.   The boots are fur lined for comfort.

21.   Her efforts were to no avail.

22.   Try to consider my feelings.

23.   Can I have a drink?

24.   That is no excuse.

25.   May I ask you a question?

26.   Most of the class enjoy football.

27.   I hope you can give me a good reason.

28.   We agree with the plan.

29.   He put on a suit.

30.   Can you tell me the value of the painting?

31.   His ship will sail into the port.

32.   Turn the wheel!

Step 4.2   Teach suffixes

Suffixes, also called endings, come at the ends of words. They can be taught through the *Snappy Lesson*™ teaching format using the flash card materials found in the *Sound Discovery*™ *Manual*, pages 81-84. The flash cards provide examples of suffixes. Students may need help with identifying all the phonemes in these suffixes. Suffixes are endings which tell the part of speech of words i.e. what job the word has in the sentence. The suffix also has a meaning which a dictionary can supply.

Phoneme splits for the suffix flash cards

s	s
es	e-s
ed	e-d or /t/ or /d/
ing	i-ng
ness	n-e-ss
ible	i-b-le
able	a-b-le
er	er
est	e-s-t
ly	l-y
age	(a-e)-g(e)
ment	m-e-n-t
ence	e-n-ce
ance	a-n-ce
ent	e-n-t
ant	a-n-t
ous	ou-s (<ou> is alt.sp. of /u/)
y	y (/i/ or /ie/)
ish	i-sh
ful	f-u-l (<u> is alt.sp. of <oo>)
al	a-l

Step 4.2 Root Words plus Suffixes for Reading and Dictation

Students may need help with:
double consonant in: controll-ed, controll-ing, controll-er, bigg-er, sadd-er, bigg-est, sadd-est, bagg-age, admitt-ance, happ-y, Mumm-y; the double consonants are pronounced once;
<y> changes to <i> in happi-ness, reli-able, happi-er, happi-est, happi-ly, marri-age, reli-ance;
long vowel sound /ie/ in tiny.
<y> is added to whole root word e.g. touch-y, love-y (where (o-e) represents the /u/ sound) except when the root word ends in a split digraph of the long vowel type: the final <e> is omitted, e.g. scar-y, rac-y.
<e> is omitted in valu-able, argu-ment, guid-ance, comput-er;
<ti> represents the /sh/ sound in infectious (further examples of the /shus/ special suffix will be given at Step 7).

suffix -s (/s/ sound)

connects	**remarks**
predicts	**loves**
breaks	**infects**
considers	**argues**
drinks	**enjoys**
agrees	**relies**

suffix -s or -es (/e/+/s/ sounds)

excuses   accesses

N.B. An <es> suffix is added after <ch> (watches) and <sh> (bushes, rushes). Note that <es> is also added after <o> (goes, pot/a/toes, tom/at/oes) to preserve the /oa/ sound.

suffix -ed (/e/+/d/ sounds) Say /e/+/d/ when the <ed> has <t> or <d> before it.

connected   predicted

infected   respected

suggested   comforted

suited   started

suffix -ed (/t/ sound) Say /t/ if the letter before <ed> is not <t> or <d> and is an **unvoiced** sound. There are occasional exceptions, like "wicked" where <e> and <d> are both pronounced.

remarked   touched

approached   liked

suffix -ed (/d/ sound) Say /d/ if the letter before the <ed> is not <t> or <d> and is a **voiced** sound. Vowel digraphs are voiced sounds, so that root words ending in vowel digraphs such as "snow" are usually followed by a /d/ sound.

loved	relied
argued	controlled
availed	considered
excused	questioned
enjoyed	reasoned
agreed	valued

suffix -ing   (when root word ends in consonant, add -ing)

connecting   approaching

drinking   agreeing

relying   enjoying

controlling   turning

suffix -ing (when root word ends in <e>, drop final <e> before adding -ing)

valuing   excusing

arguing   liking

loving

suffix -ness

likeness	kindness
happiness	sadness

suffix -ible

| accessible | suggestible |

suffix -able

remarkable	predictable
touchable	loveable
approachable	respectable
breakable	reliable

arguable	likeable
comfortable	available
considerable	drinkable
questionable	enjoyable
reasonable	agreeable
suitable	valuable

suffix -er

| lover | controller |
| questioner | valuer |

computer   teacher

porter

smaller   bigger

happier   sadder

suffix -est

smallest   biggest

happiest   saddest

suffix -ly

lovely   likely

homely	shapely
kindly	happily

suffix -age

breakage	baggage
marriage	mileage

suffix -ment

argument	enjoyment
agreement	

suffix -ence

reference   **difference**

preference   **conference**

suffix -ance

reliance   **admittance**

appearance   **guidance**

suffix -ous (/u/+/s/ sounds)

joyous   **courageous**

suffix -y (/i/ sound)

lovey   **happy**

tiny   **Mummy**

suffix -y (/ie/ sound)

rely   **my**   **sky**

suffix - ish

punish   **vanish**

suffix - ful

joyful   **respectful**

suffix - al

traditional   **professional**

Step 4.2 Sentences with Root Words plus Suffixes for Reading and Dictation

Students may need help with:

nurse, cheese	<se>	is alternative spelling pattern for the /s/ sound,
have, leave, give	<ve>	is alternative spelling pattern for the /v/ sound,
were, there	<ere>	is alternative spelling pattern for the /er/ sound,
door,	<oor>	is alternative spelling pattern for the /or/ sound,
Christmas	<st>	is alternative spelling pattern for the /s/ sound,

Irregular words are "the", "to", "was", "are", "you", "some"

suffix -s (/s/ sound)

1. This road connects the towns.

2. The remarks were true.

3. She predicts a win for her team.

4. He loves his new trainers.

5. The train breaks down.

6. The sick cat infects the man.

7. She considers the play to be too long.

8. The boy argues with his Mum.

9. She drinks a cup of tea.

10. Dad enjoys a game of cards.

11. Bob agrees with me.

12. Jane relies on her dog to keep her safe.

suffix -s or -es (/e/+/s/ sounds)

1.   He made his excuses and left.

2.   He accesses the Web from his home.

suffix -ed (/e/+/d/ sounds)   Say /e/+/d/ when the <ed> has <t> or <d> before it.

1.   The girl is well connected.

2.   He predicted the crash.

3.   The ill boy infected all his class.

4.   The vet is well respected in the town.

5.   Janet suggested how to get out.

6.   The nurse comforted the boy.

7.   It suited Mum to leave her job.

8.   The car started first time.

suffix -ed (/t/ sound)   Say /t/ if the letter before <ed> is not <t> or <d> and is an **unvoiced** sound. There are occasional exceptions, like "wicked" where <e> and <d> are both pronounced.

1.   Father remarked on my bad cold.

2.   I touched the snake.

3.   The bus approached the bus stop.

4.   We liked the film.

suffix -ed (/d/ sound) Say /d/ if the letter before the <ed> is not <t> or <d> and is a **voiced** sound. Vowel digraphs are voiced sounds, so that root words ending in vowel digraphs (such as "snow") are usually followed by a /d/ sound.

1. I loved the party.

2. We relied on our seat belts.

3. The men argued about the fish.

4. The light is controlled by this switch.

5. He availed himself of the advice given to him.

6. I considered the truth of his story.

7. She excused herself and left.

8. The teacher questioned the class.

9. We enjoyed the concert.

10. Dave reasoned with him when he was upset.

11. The rock band agreed to split.

12. The ring was valued at a thousand pounds.

suffix -ing

1. The rooms have a connecting door.

2. We saw the approaching train.

3. They went out drinking.

4.   She is agreeing with you.

5.   We are relying on his help.

6.   I was enjoying my holiday.

7.   I am controlling the speed of the car.

8.   We are valuing the house at a high price.

9.   I am not excusing him.

10.   We were arguing about the bill.

11.   He is liking his new school.

12.   I am loving this hot bath.

13.   The car is turning.

suffix -ness

1.   The portrait is a good likeness of him.

2.   Thank him for his kindness.

3.   Her happiness was clear for all to see.

4.   His death was a sadness.

suffix -ible

1.   The house on the main road is accessible.

2.   The crime upset the suggestible old man.

suffix -able

1.   That was a remarkable story.

2.   His death was predictable.

3.   The soft velvet looks touchable.

4.   New born kittens are loveable.

5.   The judge is stern but approachable.

6.   She has a respectable job.

7.   The glass is breakable.

8.   My car is reliable.

9.   His case is arguable in law.

10.   Her friend is likeable.

11.   The boots are comfortable.

12.   He is available for the job.

13.   The rich man's wealth is considerable.

14.   The cheap wine is not drinkable.

15.   His account of the crash is questionable.

16.   Fame is enjoyable.

17.   The price must be reasonable.

18.   The weather was agreeable.

19.   Her dress is suitable for the party.

20.   The plate is valuable.

suffix -er

1.   The king took a lover.

2.   He was made controller of the B.B.C.

3.   The questioner had been a spy.

4.   He was a valuer of old clocks.

5.   They liked to play on the computer.

6.   The teacher gave out the books.

7.   The porter lifts the case.

8.   This coat is smaller than mine.

9.   I have a bigger car than you.

10.   The girl is happier now that she has a job.

11.   The film is sadder than the book.

suffix -est

1.   Give me the smallest bit of ham.

2.   Let him have the biggest slice of cheese.

3.   This is the happiest time of my life.

4.   The saddest part of the play was at the end.

plus suffix -ly

1.   Those are lovely roses.

2.   He is likely to stay away.

3.   You have made the room look homely.

4.   The model has shapely legs.

5.   The kindly man gave me some help.

6.   Happily we roll along.

suffix -age

1.   The breakage rate in the bar is not too high.

2.   He took his baggage to the plane.

3.   The marriage will take place in June.

4.   The mileage of the car is ten thousand.

suffix -ment

1.   He had a bad argument with his wife.

2.   It was a day full of enjoyment.

3.   We have an agreement about the land.

suffix -ence

1.   The teacher gave the boy a job reference.

2.   His pay rise will make a difference.

3.   Can I state my preference?

4.   We shall hold the next conference in Leeds.

suffix -ance

1. He did not place much reliance on her story.

2. There is an admittance charge of five pounds.

3. Her appearance in the film made her a star.

4. The therapist gave the girl some guidance.

suffix -ous (/u/+/s/ sounds)

1. I hope you have a joyous Christmas.

2. The brave boy did a courageous thing.

suffix -y (/i/ sound)

1. The film star said, "Sit down, lovey."

2. I am happy to see you.

3. Sam had the part of Tiny Tim in the play.

4. Mummy came to meet me.

suffix -y (/ie/ sound)

1. They rely on Dad to help them.

2. My first job is to clean the hall.

3. The new girl was shy.

suffix - ish

1.   The state will punish him for his crime.

2.   The wizard made him vanish.

suffix - ful

1.   They sang a joyful song.

2.   We stand in a respectful way in church.

suffix - al

1.   We had a traditional Christmas.

2.   He is a professional golfer.

Step 4.3   Teach prefixes

Prefixes come at the beginning of words. Prefixes can be taught through the *Snappy Lesson*™ teaching
format using the flash card materials found in the *Sound Discovery Manual*, pages 85-86. The flash cards
provide examples of prefixes. Students may need help with identifying all the phonemes in these prefixes.

Phoneme splits for the prefix flash cards

	phonemes
in	i-n
trans	t-r-a-n-s
mis	m-i-s
un	u-n
pre	p-r-e
post	p-o-s-t
sub	s-u-b
pro	p-r-o
dis	d-i-s
im	i-m
re	r-e
ex	e-x

Prefixes can add to or change the meaning of words. Most prefixes are Latin prepositions. About fifty
percent of our words come from Latin, the language of the Romans, and ten to twelve percent come from
Anglo-Saxon, the language of England during the early Middle Ages. Students may find it helpful to know
about the meanings of prefixes:

in	in, into, not
trans	across
mis	wrong, bad, erroneous (Anglo-Saxon)
un	not, contrary to, opposite of (Anglo-Saxon)
pre	before
post	after
sub	under
pro	for/in favour of, acting as a substitute for, before/forward (in time or position)
dis	apart from, reversal, not
im	(like in-) in, into, not
re	back, again
ex	out of, outside of, from, former

Step 4.3 Root Words plus Prefixes for Reading and Spelling

prefix in-

infect **inject** **inhuman**

prefix trans-

transport **transfer**

prefix mis-

misspell **mischief**

prefix un-

unlike **unhappy** **unkind**

prefix pre-

predict **prefer** **prefect**

prefix post-

postpone **postscript**

prefix sub-

subway   **submit**

prefix pro-

profession   **progress**

prefix dis-

disconnect   **disinfect**

discourage   **dislike**

discomfort   **disagree**

prefix im-

import

prefix re-

report   **return**

reconect   **reinfect**

prefix ex-

export

Step 4.3 Sentences with Root Words plus Prefixes for Reading and Dictation

Students may need help with:
nurse,   <se> is alternative spelling pattern for the /s/ sound,
were, there   <ere> is alternative spelling pattern for the /er/ sound,
floor   <oor> is alternative spelling pattern for the /or/ sound,
Irregular words are "the", "to", "do", "into", "was", "you", "some"

prefix in-

1.   A bite from that rat may infect you.

2.   The nurse came to inject the sick man.

3.   The war camps were inhuman.

prefix trans-

1.   I need transport to get to town.

2.   The football player will transfer to a new club.

prefix mis-

1.   Do not misspell my name.

2.   The boys got into mischief.

prefix un-

1.   She is unlike her Mum.

2.   The sad song made her unhappy.

3.   That was an unkind thing to do.

prefix pre-

1.	They predict you will win.

2.	I prefer white wine to red.

3.	He was made a prefect at school.

prefix post-

1.	Can you postpone the party until next week?

2.	There was a postscript at the end of the letter.

prefix sub-

1.	There is a subway in New York.

2.	We had to submit a claim for the land.

prefix pro-

1.	If you study you can enter a profession.

2.	He makes good progress.

prefix dis-

1.	He needs to disconnect the power.

2.	Will you disinfect the toilet?

3.	Do not discourage the boy.

4.   I dislike custard.

5.   He slept on the floor in some discomfort.

6.   I disagree with that point.

prefix im-

1.   We import rice and tea.

prefix re-

1.   Her school report was bad.

2.   Will you return my bag?

prefix ex-

1.   They export ships.

Step 4.3 Root Words plus Suffixes and Prefixes for Reading and Spelling

prefix in-, suffix -ed

infected

prefix in-, suffix -ible

inaccessible

prefix in-, suffix -ate

inconsiderate

prefix in-, suffix -able

inexcusable   invaluable

prefix un-, suffix -able

unremarkable untouchable

unapproachable

unbreakable   unreliable

uncontrollable unlikeable

undrinkable   unsuitable

unreasonable predictable

unpredictable disagreeable

prefix un-, suffix -al

unprofessional

prefix dis-, suffix -ing

disconnecting

prefix dis-, suffix -ant

disinfectant

prefix dis-, suffix -ment

discouragement

prefix dis-, suffix -s

dislikes

prefix im-, suffix -ant

important

prefix im-, suffix -er

importer

prefix ex-, suffix -er

exporter

prefix re-, suffix -er

reporter

prefix re-, suffix -ing

returning

Step 4.3 Sentences with Root Words, plus Suffixes and Prefixes for Reading and Spelling

Students may need help with:
Irregular words "the", "was".

prefix in-, suffix -ed

1.　　　The cut was infected.

prefix in-, suffix -ible

1.　　　The town was inaccessible.

prefix in-, suffix -ate

1.　　　His boss is inconsiderate.

prefix in-, suffix -able

1.　　　Her lie is inexcusible.

2.　　　His help was invaluable.

3.　　　The play was unremarkable.

4.　　　The hot plate is untouchable.

5.　　　The angry dog was unapproachable.

6.　　　The glass is unbreakable.

7.　　　The car is unreliable.

8.	His rage was uncontrollable.

9.	It is sad that she is unlikeable.

10.	The sweet tea is undrinkable.

11.	The coat was unsuitable.

12.	He was being unreasonable.

13.	The weather was unpredictable.

14.	The man was disagreeable.

prefix un-, suffix -al

1.	To talk to the press would be unprofessional.

prefix dis-, suffix -ing

1.	His smile was disconcerting.

2.	Clean the sink with disinfectant!

prefix dis-, suffix -ment

1.	His low marks were a discouragement.

2.	She had her likes and dislikes.

prefix im-, suffix -ant

1.	He is an important man.

prefix im-, suffix -er

1.	His wife is an importer.

prefix ex-, suffix -er

1.	My boss is an exporter of soft toys.

prefix re-, suffix -er

1.	Bob is a reporter on The Times.

prefix re-, suffix -ing

1.	When is Jim returning home?

STEP 5   TEACH SYLLABLE TYPES

In order to separate words into syllables it is useful to know about the different types of syllables which are found in words. There are 6 kinds of syllables:

Where:

V =		vowel
C =		consonant
e =		letter <e>
I =		letter <I>
R =		letter <r>

Step 5.1 closed   VC

In closed syllables: the letter <a> represents the /a/ sound
the letter <e> represents the /e/ sound
the letter <I> represents the /i/ sound
the letter <o> represents the /o/ sound
the letter <u> represents the /u/ sound

Step 5.2 vowel consonant-e   VCe

Step 5.3 open   CV

In open syllables: the letter <a> represents the /ai/ sound
the letter <e> represents the /ee/ sound
the letter <i> represents the /ie/ sound
the letter <o> represents the /oa/ sound
the letter <u> represents the /ue/ sound

Step 5.4 vowel combination   V V

Also some consonants can act as vowels when they join with a vowel to produce a single sound/phoneme: e.g. <aw> as in lawn, <ow> as in snow, <igh> as in light, <oul> as in could.

Step 5.5 consonant-le   Cle

Step 5.6 vowel controlled r   VR

These syllable types can be taught through the *Snappy Lesson*™ teaching format using the flash card materials found in the *Sound Discovery*™ *Manual*, pages 87-92. The flash cards provide examples of each type of syllable. By this stage of the programme students should be able to identify all the phonemes in these syllables and then blend them for reading or segment them for spelling.

Step 5.1   Closed Syllable Words for Reading and Dictation

For more information about closed syllables see *Sound Discovery™ Manua*l: Teaching Framework - Step 5. For more examples of closed syllable, 3 phoneme CVC words for Reading and Dictation see *Sound Discovery™ Words and Sentences Steps 1 to 3*, Step 1.1.

pan   **tin**   **let**

rod   **fun**

Step 5.1   Sentences with Closed Syllable Words for Reading and Dictation

For more examples of sentences containing closed syllable, 3 phoneme CVC words for Reading and Dictation see *Sound Discovery™ Words and Sentences Steps 1 to 3*, Step 1.1.

1. The pan is hot.

2. He hit the tin.

3. Mum let her sit up.

4. Did he tap the rod?

5. We had fun.

Step 5.2   Vowel-Consonant-e Syllable Words for Reading and Dictation

For more information about vowel-consonant-e syllables see *Sound Discovery™ Manual: Teaching Framework - Step 5*. For more examples of Vce syllable words as main alternative vowel spellings for Reading and Dictation see *Sound Discovery™ Words and Sentences Steps 1 to 3*, Step 3A.2, Step 3A.3, Step 3 A.4, Step 3A.5, and Step 3A.6.

ate　　**these**　　**like**

home　　**huge**

Step 5.2   Sentences with Vowel-Consonant -e Syllable Words for Reading and Dictation

For more examples of sentences containing Vce syllable words as main alternative vowel spellings for Reading and Dictation see *Sound Discovery™ Words and Sentences Steps 1 to 3*, Step 3A.2, Step 3A.3, Step 3A.4, Step 3A.5, and Step 3A.6.

1. He ate the cake.

2. These themes are complete.

3. I like my bike.

4. We hope he is close to home.

5. Can I use this huge tube?

Step 5.3   Open Syllable Words for Reading and Dictation

For more information about open syllables see *Sound Discovery™ Manual: Teaching Framework - Step 5*.
For more examples of open syllable words see *Sound Discovery™ Words and Sentences Steps 1 to 3*, Step 3.
In open syllables <a> represents the /ai/ sound, <e> the /ee/ sound, <i > the /ie/ sound, <o> the /oa/ sound and <u> the /ue/ sound.

vacant   refuse   silent

open   unite

Step 5.3   Sentences with Open Syllable Words for Reading and Dictation

For more examples of sentences with open syllable words see *Sound Discovery™ Words and Sentences Steps 1 to 3*, Step 3.

1. A job on the paper is vacant.

2. She will refuse to be a decoy.

3. The pilot had a silent landing.

4. The robot is going to open up.

5. He has the skill to unite the units.

Step 5.4   Vowel Combination Syllable Words for Reading and Dictation

For more information about vowel combination syllables see *Sound Discovery*™ *Manual*: Teaching Framework - Step 5. For more examples of vowel combination syllable words see *Sound Discovery*™ *Words and Sentences Steps 1 to 3*, Step 2.2, Step 2.4 and Step 3A.

sail	strain	paint
bee	sheep	seeds
lie	tries	fried
boat	coach	float
cue	coin	point
joint	ouch	loud
sound	cook	shook
moon	tooth	shoot
day	stay	they
grey	meat	speak
please	light	fright

show	throw	few
stew	Paul	sauce
haunt	jaw	shawl
prawn	all	small
talk	chalk	boy
cow	down	brown
would	should	blue
true	blew	screw
you	soup	dead
bread	said	friend
touch	young	

Note that if these vowels appear in reverse order, they no longer have a single sound. Usually, each will have its own sound: a long sound in an open syllable, a short sound in a closed syllable.

cha os   ne on   the or y   di ar y   gi ant

li ar   vi o let   vi o lin   tri umph   tru ant

Step 5.4   Sentences with Vowel Combination Syllable Words for Reading and Dictation

For more examples of sentences with vowel combination syllable words see *Sound Discovery*™ *Words and Sentences Steps 1 to 3*, Step 2.2, Step 2.4 and Step 3A.

1. They will sail to Spain.

2. Push now but try not to strain.

3. Can you paint the rail?

4. The bee went to its hive.

5. The sheep ate the grass.

6. He planted the seeds in the pot.

7. Do not tell me a lie.

8. He tries hard.

9. We like fried bacon and eggs.

10. The boat went out to sea.

11. He drove the coach to London.

12. The cork will float on the water.

13. That is my cue to leave.

14   Can you lend me a pound coin?

15.   It is not polite to point.

16.   They had a joint of pork for lunch.

17.   He said, "Ouch!" as the stone hit him.

18.   The band was loud.

19.   She did not make a sound.

20.   Dad is not a bad cook.

21.   He shook the tin.

22.   The moon will come out soon.

23.   He lost a tooth when Bob hit him.

24.   Try to shoot at the target.

25.   The day was wet.

26.   Can you not stay for breakfast?

27.   They went out to the pub.

28.   His hair went grey.

29.   The meat tasted good.

30.   I wish to speak to you.

31.   Please come home.

32.   Could you give me a light?

33.   The loud bang gave me a fright.

34.   Will you show him the way to the shops?

35.   Just throw it away.

36.   A few children were late for school.

37.   The meat stew was good.

38.   Paul can do it.

39.   I made a sauce for the chicken.

40.   His ghost will haunt you.

41.   He hit his jaw on the ground when he fell.

42.   You will need your shawl tonight.

43.   Gran loves prawn cocktail.

44.   All the food was eaten.

45.   The small boy fell from the swing.

46.   It is good to talk.

47.   She drew with chalk on the playground.

48.   The boy walked along the wall.

49.   The cow became sick.

50.   Will you sit down.

51.   Dad brushed his brown shoes.

52.   Would you go to the shops for me?

53.   Should he be let in without a ticket?

54.   Blue, blue, my life is blue.

55.   It was a true story.

56.   The wind blew the flag.

57.   A screw came loose.

58.   You need to help me.

59.   You can open a tin of soup.

60.   His parents are dead.

61.   Can you toast some bread?

62.   He said he would come back.

63.   My friend came with me.

64.   Do not touch the hot plate!

65.   She is too young for this class.

Vowels in reverse order which have their own sounds in words of more than one syllable

1.   The traffic was in chaos.

2.   The street was lit by neon lights.

3.   He passed his theory test.

4.   She kept a diary.

5.   The giant climbed the bean stalk.

6.   Are you calling me a liar?

7.   There were violets in the wood.

8.   She plays the violin.

9.   The army came home in triumph.

10.   He played truant from school.

Step 5.5   Consonant-l-e Syllable Words for Reading and Dictation

For more information about consonant-l-e syllables see *Sound Discovery*™ *Manual*: Teaching Framework - Step 5. Consonant-l-e comes at the end of words. Since the <e> is always silent, the syllable lacks a vowel sound. <le> can be considered an alternative spelling of the /l/ sound. To cut off this type of syllable, count back three letters, beginning with the <e>: thim/ble, sta/ple. The following words are all two syllable words:

closed syllable words - (note that the vowel sound is "short". With a single consonant and a single vowel the consonant doubles in order to retain the closed syllable with a "short" vowel sound. e.g. for bubble - double the consonant; for sample - no need to double. Note also that in "double" the short vowel sound /u/ is achieved by the alternative spelling <ou>. The short vowel sound /u/ is preserved in the syllable split - dou/ble- and hence it is not necessary to double the consonant <b>.)

bubble	**ruffle**	**double**
puzzle	**apple**	**dwindle**
riddle	**dribble**	**trample**
simple	**kettle**	**ripple**
dimple	**whittle**	**spittle**
crumple	**rattle**	**ankle**
little	**jingle**	**rumple**
twinkle	**topple**	**juggle**
crackle	**throttle**	**bottle**
buckle	**wrinkle**	**wriggle**
shingle	**bangle**	**sample**
thimble		

Note: j-i-n(g)/gle, b-a-n(g)/gle. sh-i-n(g)/gle, an(g)/kle, t-w-i-n(g)/kle

open syllable words (note that the vowel sound is "long")

able	stable	rifle
trifle	bugle	cable
table	cradle	maple
staple	beetle	

words with the consonants <st> before the <l>.

In these words the <t> has no sound. We hear only /s/+/l/ e.g. wrestle = r-e-s-l,
nestle = n-e-s-l. <st> can be considered as an alternative spelling of the /s/ sound.

wrestle	castle	hustle
thistle	whistle	trestle
bustle	jostle	pestle
rustle	gristle	nestle
bristle		

Step 5.5   Sentences with Consonant-l-e Syllable Words for Reading and Dictation

For more information about consonant-l-e syllables see *Sound Discovery*™ *Manual*: Teaching Framework - Step 5.

closed syllable words (note that the vowel sound is "short")

1.   He blew a bubble.

2.   I saw the duck ruffle its feathers.

3.   When you double three you get nine.

4.   The boys play with the puzzle.

5.   A man ate the apple.

6.   Try not to dwindle your savings away.

7.   The wise man solved the riddle.

8.   The baby still dribbles.

9.   The cows trampled the cowslips.

10.   Keep it simple!

11.   Will you boil a kettle.

12.   The stone made ripples on the lake.

13.   You have a dimple on your chin.

14.   Boys used to whittle sticks with a knife.

15.   The spittle ran down her face.

16.   Silk crumples easily.

17.   The baby shook the rattle.

18.   David broke his ankle.

19.   You should study little and often.

20.   They sang "Jingle Bells".

21.   You will rumple the sheets on the bed.

22.   She played, "Twinkle, Twinkle Little Star."

23.   The pile of bricks began to topple.

24.   I can juggle with six balls.

25.   His breakfast went, "Snap, crackle and pop!"

26.   If you press the throttle the car will go faster.

27.   He drank a bottle of milk.

28.   The belt had a big buckle.

29.   The face cream helped her wrinkles.

30.   Do not wriggle around so much.

31.   They walked along the shingle.

32.   She has a gold bangle.

33.   This is a sample for you to try.

34.   She lost her thimble.

open syllable words (note that the vowel sound is "long")

1. I am able to swim.
2. The new foal is in the stable.
3. He shot the deer with his rifle.
4. They like to eat trifle.
5. He is proud of his bugle.
6. The cable snapped.
7. They all sat at the table.
8. The baby was in the cradle.
9. The maple tree gives a nice syrup.
10. Rice is their staple diet.

words with consonants <st> before the <l>. In these words the <t> has no sound.

1. The two men began to fight and wrestle.
2. The King and Queen lived in a castle.
3. You need to hustle the crowd to safety.
4. The thistle grows in Scotland.
5. Can you whistle this tune?
6. We set up a trestle table for the party.
7. There was a lot of bustle in the market.
8. Do not jostle me!
9. Grind the spices with a pestle and mortar!
10. There was rustle of dried leaves.
11. The meat was full of gristle.
12. The baby liked to nestle next to its mother.
13. He swept the patio with a bristle brush.

Step 5.6   r- Combination Syllable Words for Reading and Dictation

The r-combination syllable consists of each of the single vowels followed by an <r>. For more information about r-combination syllable words see *Sound Discovery™ Manual*: Teaching Framework - Step 5. For more examples of r-combination syllable words see *Sound Discovery™ Words and Sentences Steps 1 to 3*, Step 2.3 and Step 3A.7.

part   spark   start   star

term   nerve   mixer   her

girl   dirt   stir

fork   corn   for

burn   curl   fur

Step 5.6　Sentences with r- Combination Syllable Words for Reading and Dictation

For more examples of r-combination syllable words see *Sound Discovery™ Words and Sentences Steps 1 to 3, Step 2.3 and Step 3A.7.*

1.　She has a big part in the play.

2.　The spark plugs are damp.

3.　Can you start the car?

4.　I think it is a planet and not a star.

5.　Term begins next week.

6.　You have a nerve to ask me that.

7.　My food mixer helps me with cooking.

8.　Will you help her to get home?

9.　The girl swam in the sea.

10.　Clean the dirt from his boots!

11.　You must stir the soup.

12.　I can pick up the peas with my fork.

13.　She feeds corn to her hens.

14.　What are you waiting for?

15.　That flame will burn you.

16.　The leaf began to curl.

17.　The cat licks its fur.

r-combination syllables: ar, er, ir, or, and ur

r-combinations produce various sounds. The key to the vowel sound of these syllables is **the letter following** the <r>.

- Each of the r-controlled syllables on page 63 is both a vowel digraph and a single phoneme. Single phonemes are found when a consonant other than <r> follows the <r> of the r-controlled syllable or when the r-controlled syllable is at the end of some words. <ar> and <or> are separate single phonemes with different sounds, as in **far** and **for**. <er>, <ir> and <ur> are different spellings of the same phoneme /er/ which all represent the same sound, as in **her, girl, burn.**

However, note the following:

- When <ar> and <or> are endings they represent the same phoneme - /er/, as in:

collar   doctor   mixer

- When the letter <r> follows the <r> of an r-controlled syllable, the r-controlled vowel is short. The Vr combination represents two separate phonemes and the first syllable acts like a closed syllable with a "protected" short vowel sound:

carry	**carrot**	**merry**	**errand**	**mirror**	**borrow**	
c-a-rr-y	c-a-rr-o-t	m-e-rr-y	e-rr-a-n-d	m-i-rr-o-r	b-o-rr-ow	– phoneme splits
car/ry	car/rot	mer/ry	er/rand	mir/ror	bor/row	– syllable splits

- When there is a vowel after the <r> of the r-controlled syllable, the r-controlled vowel may either represent the long or the short sound. The vowel and the letter <r> act as separate phonemes:

*The Vr vowels are "unprotected" and have the **long** vowel sound of an open syllable.*

vary	**fury**	**erupt**	**glory**		
v-a-r-y	f-u-r-y	e-r-u-p-t	g-l-o-r-y		– phoneme splits
va/ry	fu/ry	e/rupt	glo/ry		– syllable splitts

era	**serious**	**hero**	**siren**	**borax**	
e-r-a	s-e-r-i-ou-s	h-e-r-o	s-i-r-e-n	b-o-r-a-x	– phoneme splits
e/ra	se/ri/ous	he/ro	si/ren	bo/rax	– ayllable splits

N.B. This is not the case with the following:

*The Vr vowels are "protected" and have the **short** vowel sound of a closed syllable.*

very	**peril**	**carol**	
v-e-r-y	p-e-r-i-l	c-a-r-o-l	– phoneme splits
ver/y	per/il	car/ol	– syllable spits

Step 6 Teach Syllable Division
in Polysyllabic Words

Syllable division in polysyllabic words can be taught as it relates to the known syllable types through the *Snappy Lesson*™ teaching format using the flash card materials found in the *Sound Discovery*™ *Manual*, pages 87-92, and the materials provided above at Step 5. For more information about teaching syllable division see *Sound Discovery*™ *Manual:* Teaching Framework - Step 5.

Syllable division in polysyllabic words is taught for each syllable type as follows:

Step 6.1   Closed syllables

Step 6.2   Vowel consonant-e syllables

Step 6.3   Open syllables

Step 6.4   Vowel combination syllables

Step 6.5   Consonant-l-e syllables

Step 6.6   r-combination syllables

The order of difficulty for teaching each syllable type is as follows:

- two syllable words, with no more than 3 phonemes per syllable

- two syllable words, with more than 3 phonemes in at least one syllable

- three or more syllable words

Step 6.1   Closed Syllable Words for Reading and Dictation

For more examples of closed syllable, 3 phoneme CVC compound words for Reading and Dictation see *Sound Discovery™ Words and Sentences Steps 1 to 3*, Step 1.2.

> ## Two syllable words, no more than three phonemes per syllable, for Reading and Dictation

split between compound words

sunset   **hatpin**

split between two like consonants

rabbit   **gossip**

Beware of words containing <cc>. This is not a digraph. In the following word the first <c> represents the /c/ sound and the second <c> represents the /s/ sound as it is followed by <e>. <ss> represents the /s/ sound and is one phoneme.

success   *suc/cess*

split between two consonants

combat   **discuss**

one consonant only - split after closed syllable

solid   **melon**   **dragon**

consonant digraph - do not split digraph

rocket   **ethnic**   **chitchat**

Two syllable words, more than 3 phonemes in at least one syllable, for Reading and Dictation

split between two consonants

consent

plastic

trumpet

disrupt

invent

split between two like consonants

comment

Beware of words containing <cc>. This is not a digraph. In the following word the first <c> represents the /c/ sound and the second <c> represents the /s/ sound as it is followed by <e>:

accept

ac/cept

3 consonants - cluster usually (but not always) goes with second syllable

hundred

dentist

contract

subtract

scoundrel

pumpkin

but pump/kin

2/2:

handclasp   **grandstand**

do not split digraph:

wingspan   **pamphlet**

mischief   **within**

bathtub   **singsong**

1/3:

obstruct   **instruct**

Three or more syllable words for Reading and Dictation

split according to above principles:

kinesthetic   kin/es/thet/ic

fantastic   fan/tas/tic

athletic   ath/let/ic

principal   prin/cip/al

hospital   hos/pit/al

president   pres/id/ent

establish   es/tab/lish

symbolic   sym/bol/ic

capital   cap/it/al

mechanical   mech/an/ic/al

Beware of words containing <cc>. They do not contain a digraph. In the following word the first <c> represents the /c/ sound and the second <c> represents the /s/ sound as it is followed by <i>:

accident   ac/cid/ent

Step 6.1   Sentences with Closed Syllable Words for Reading and Dictation

For more examples of setences with closed syllable, 3 phoneme CVC compound words for Reading and Dictation see *Sound Discovery™ Words and Sentences Steps 1 to 3*, Step 1.2.

> Two syllable words, no more than three phonemes per syllable, for Reading and Dictation

1. Last night there was a lovely sunset.

2. Mum stuck a hatpin into her hat.

3. They kept a rabbit in a hutch.

4. You should not gossip.

5. His success came late in life.

6. The two men were locked in combat.

7. Let us discuss this problem together.

8. The statue was made of solid metal.

9. He cut the melon into six bits.

10. The dragon story is just a myth.

11. The rocket shot up into the sky.

12. Her outfit had an ethnic theme.

13. We enjoy a chitchat when we meet.

Two syllable words, more than 3 phonemes in at least one syllable, for Reading and Dictation

split between two consonants

1. Mum did not give her consent for me to go.
2. Mobile phones often disrupt meetings.
3. My plastic raincoat kept me dry in the rain.
4. He tries to invent new things.
5. She plays the trumpet in a band.

split between two like consonants

1. Your comment about the meeting was helpful.
2. I cannot accept his gift.

3 consonants - cluster usually (but not always) goes with second syllable

1. She won a hundred pounds.
2. When you subtract three from ten you get seven.
3. I went to the dentist with my bad tooth.
4. The man who stole the money is a scoundrel.
5. The film star has a contract to act in Holywood.
6. Pumpkin pie is too sweet for me.

4 consonants can split variously

1. He gave me a strong handclasp.
2. We saw the football match from the grandstand.
3. That seagull has a large wingspan.
4. I read the pamphlet about healthy food.
5. The boy got up to mischief.
6. There is a lot of talent within his family.
7. She lay in the hot bathtub.
8. Coming back in the coach we had a singsong.
9. The fallen tree will obstruct the cycle path.
10. I will instruct him to go to the bank for us.

split according to above principles

1. Kinesthetic help uses the body's position in space.

2. The party was fantastic.

3. The football team are all athletic.

4. He is the principal of the college.

5. The boxer had to be taken to hospital.

6. He is the President of Brazil.

7. They tried to establish a new school in the town.

8. The use of bread and wine in church is symbolic.

9. The capital of Ireland is Dublin.

10. The car has a mechanical problem.

11. He had an accident on his boat.

Step 6.2 Vowel Consonant-e Syllable Words for Reading and Dictation

For more examples of vowel consonant-e compound words for Reading and Dictation see *Sound Discovery™ Words and Sentences Steps 1 to 3*, Step 3.

> Two syllable words, no more than three phonemes per syllable for Reading and Dictation

dislike	despite
tadpole	mistake
dispute	compete
expose	trombone

> Two syllable words, more than 3 phonemes in at least one syllable for Reading and Dictation

complete	inflate
explode	bracelet
include	explore
translate	subscribe

legislate   leg/is/late

hesitate   hes/it/ate

navigate   nav/ig/ate

celebrate   cel/eb/rate

escapade   es/cap/ade

centigrade   cen/tig/rade

incomplete   in/com/plete

constitute   con/stit/ute (2nd <t> = /ch/)

gratitude   grat/it/ude (2nd <t> = /ch/)

criticise   crit/ic/ise (2nd <c> = /s/)

aggravate   ag/grav/ate

Step 6.2 Sentences with Vowel Consonant-e Syllable Words for Reading and Dictation

For more examples of sentences with vowel consonant-e compound words for Reading and Dictation see *Sound Discovery™ Words and Sentences Steps 1 to 3*, Step 3.

> ## Two syllable words, no more than three phonemes per syllable for Reading and Dictation

1. We dislike exams.
2. He did the job despite being ill.
3. The tadpole swam in the jar.
4. I made a mistake.
5. My boss had a dispute with his men.
6. The boy likes to compete and to win.
7. Low tide will expose the rocks.
8. Bob likes to play his trombone.

> ## Two syllable words, more than 3 phonemes in at least one syllable for Reading and Dictation

1. Let us complete the game.
2. This pump will inflate the football.
3. The bombs began to explode.
4. Her bracelet was solid gold.
5. You need to include Janet.
6. Can we explore the old house?
7. My job is to translate this into French.
8. Do you subscribe to the newspaper?

Three or more syllable words for
Reading and Dictation

1.   MPs legislate in the House of Commons.

2.   Do not hesitate when you start.

3.   The sailor can navigate by the stars.

4.   They went out to celebrate.

5.   The escapade ended in disaster.

6.   It was twenty degrees centigrade.

7.   The book is incomplete.

8.   Ten players consitute the team.

9.   She sent a letter in gratitude.

10.   I will not criticise you.

11.   Did the shouting aggravate you?

Step 6.3 — Open Syllable Words for Reading and Dictation

For more examples of open syllable compound words for Reading and Dictation see *Sound Discovery*™ *Words and Sentences Steps 1 to 3*, Step 3.

Two syllable words, no more than three phonemes per syllable for Reading and Dictation

final	music	tiny
broken	sloping	even
legal		

Two syllable words, more than 3 phonemes in at least one syllable for Reading and Dictation

| silent | protect | recent |
| secret | April | student |

Three or more syllable words for Reading and Dictation

compliant com/pli/ant

calculate cal/cu/late

elephant	el/e/phant
antelope	an/te/lope
electric	e/lec/tric
crocodile	croc/o/dile
saturate	sat/u/rate
telephone	tel/e/phone
dynamite	dy/nam/ite (<y> = /ie/)
microscope	mi/cros/cope
microphone	mi/croph/one (<ph> = /f/)
monument	mon/u/ment
acrobat	ac/ro/bat
consequence	con/se/quence(2nd <c> = /s/)
accumulate	ac/cu/mu/late (both <c> = /c/)

Step 6.3 Sentences with Open Syllable Words for Reading and Dictation

For more examples of sentences with open syllable compound words for Reading and Dictation see *Sound Discovery™ Words and Sentences Steps 1 to 3*, Step 3.

> ## Two syllable words, no more than three phonemes per syllable for Reading and Dictation

1. This is the final page of the book.

2. Do you like pop music?

3. The tiny baby went to sleep.

4. He had a broken leg.

5. He fell on the sloping path.

6. Even the boys cried.

7. The document is legal.

> ## Two syllable words, more than 3 phonemes in at least one syllable for Reading and Dictation

1. The street was silent at night.

2. I shall try to protect you.

3. His recent trip was to Spain.

4. Can you keep a secret?

5. April comes after March.

6. He is a student at the school.

| | Three or more syllable words for
Reading and Dictation |

1.   He was a compliant team member.

2.   I can calculate how much it will cost.

3.   We saw an elephant in the zoo.

4.   The antelope has a smooth skin.

5.   The old house now has electric light.

6.   A crocodile swam in the river.

7.   The rain will saturate the lawn.

8.   The telephone rang.

9.   They blew up the rock face with dynamite.

10.   You can see the virus under the microscope.

11.   Can you turn on the microphone?

12.   There was a monument in the park.

13.   The acrobat ran across the tightrope.

14.   The mistake is of no consequence.

15.   You need to accumulate some money.

Step 6.4 Vowel Combination Syllable Words for Reading and Dictation

For more examples of vowel combination compound words for Reading and Dictation see *Sound Discovery™ Words and Sentences Steps 1 to 3*, Step 2.2, Step 2.4 and Step 3.

Two syllable words, no more than three phonemes per syllable for Reading and Dictation

maiden	regain
boiling	shampoo
enjoy	peanut
mushroom	twilight
poison	yellow
raincoat	Tuesday
rescue	afloat
feeding	oilcan
boasted	football
woollen	heaven
haunted	coachman

leapfrog	sneezing
spoonful	applaud
scoundrel	crouching
soundproof	ointment
trainee	toasted
freezing	friendship
frighten	August
greyhound	crispbread
breakfast	sweetpea
clueless	

Three or more syllable words for Reading and Dictation	

enlighten	en/ligh/ten
dinosaur	di/no/saur
appointee	ap/poin/tee
celluloid	cell/u/loid
continue	con/tin/ue
walkabout	walk/ab/out
roundabout	roun/dab/out
unfriendly	un/friend/ly
chimpanzee	chim/pan/zee
astronaut	as/tro/naut
enjoyment	en/joy/ment
refugee	ref/u/gee (<g> = /j/ sound)
reproachful	re/proach/ful

Step 6.4 Sentences with Vowel Combination Syllable Words for Reading and Dictation

For more examples of sentences with vowel combination compound words for Reading and Dictation see *Sound Discovery™ Words and Sentences Steps 1 to 3*, Step 2.2, Step 2.4 and Step 3.

Two syllable words, no more than three phonemes per syllable for Reading and Dictation

1. The fairy tale was about a maiden.
2. He had to rest to regain his health.
3. The pot was boiling.
4. I like herb shampoo.
5. We enjoy good music.
6. He had a peanut bar for his snack.
7. Mum made a mushroom omlette.
8. The bats came out at twilight.
9. They had to poison the rats.
10. She wore a yellow oilskin.
11. You should take your raincoat.
12. We leave on Tuesday.
13. The lifeboat came to the rescue.
14. His life jacket kept him afloat.
15. The chicks need a lot of feeding.
16. He filled the oilcan with the best oil.
17. He boasted that he had won.
18. The football team came first.
19. His woollen jumper got wet.
20. This icecream is heaven.
21. The house is haunted.
22. The coachman took us to the ball.

Two syllable words, more than 3 phonemes in at least one syllable for Reading and Dictation

1. The children played leapfrog.

2. They began sneezing in the dusty room.

3. You need a spoonful of cod liver oil.

4. We can applaud him when he finishes.

5. The scoundrel stole my handbag.

6. The cat was crouching on the ground.

7. He recorded the tape in a soundproof room.

8. Let me put ointment on the cut.

9. She is a trainee teacher.

10. I like toasted crumpets.

11. It is freezing outside.

12. The present is a mark of our friendship.

13. The vet tries not to frighten the kitten.

14. We go on holiday in August.

15. The greyhound ran fast round the track.

16. We ate cheese and crispbread for lunch.

17. Give us bacon and egg for breakfast!

18. Our sweetpea plants have done well.

19. You are clueless!

Three or more syllable words for Reading and Dictation

1. Please enlighten me with your wisdom.

2. The dinosaur fossil was found in the rock.

3. The new appointee to the job is from Bristol.

4. The film reel was made of celluloid.

5. Can you continue singing.

6. The Queen went on a walkabout.

7. The car got lost at the roundabout.

8. The class was unfriendly to the new pupil.

9. The baby chimpanzee was a good size.

10. The astronaut was first to walk on the moon.

11. The band gave so much enjoyment.

12. He is a refugee from Afganistan.

13. The sick child gave me a reproachful look.

Step 6.5   Consonant-l-e Syllable Words
for Reading and Dictation

Step 5.5 gives examples of two syllable consonant-l-e words: closed syllable words, open syllable words and words containing <stle>. Please refer to section Step 5.5 for examples of two syllable words, pages 58-59.

Three or more syllable words for Reading and Dictation

compound words

simpleton	sim/ple/ton
kettledrum	ket/tle/drum .
mettlesome	met/tle/some
Littlewoods	lit/tle/woods
anklebone	an(g)/kle/bone
bottleneck	bot/tle/neck
stableboy	sta/ble/boy
tabletop	ta/ble/top
Stapleton	sta/ple/ton
thistledown	thistle/down

Words derived from consonant-l-e words split in a different way. The split comes between the consonant and the <l>, the <e> is omitted and a suffix is added - C/l (e) + suffix:

littlest   litt/lest

puzzling   puzz/ling

trampled   tramp/led   where <ed> = /d/

doublet   doub/let

doubloon   doub/loon

Step 6.5 Sentences with Consonant-l-e Syllable Words for Reading and Dictation

Step 5.5 gives examples of sentences with two syllable consonant-l-e words: closed syllable words, open syllable words and words containing <stle>. Please refer to section Step 5.5 for examples of sentences using two syllable words, pages 60-62.

> ## Three or more syllable words for Reading and Dictation

compound words

1. Simple Simon was a simpleton.

2. The drummer played the kettledrum.

3. The winning horse is mettlesome.

4. The Littlewoods store is on High Street.

5. He broke his anklebone.

6. The stableboy gave the horse some hay.

7. We played tabletop games.

8. We live on Stapleton Road.

9. The dress was as soft as thistledown.

derived words

1. The littlest puppy died.

2. The mystery was puzzling.

3. The goats trampled grass.

4. The actor had to put on a doublet.

5. They found a Spanish doubloon.

Step 6.6   r- Combination Syllable Words for Reading and Dictation

Step 5.6 gives further explanations of r-combination syllables and should be referred to.

<ar>

> Two syllable words, no more than three phonemes per syllable for Reading and Dictation

<ar> sounds /ar/ , one phoneme, when followed by consonant other than <r>

farmyard	parting	target
market	garden	carpet
harness	scarlet	carbon
marble	garbage	garlic
party	army	startle	tardy

<ar> sounds /er/, one phoneme, in the final syllable of words. Spelling tip: say word as it is spelt.

mustard	blizzard	collar
beggar	pillar	

<ar> sounds /a/+/r/, two phonemes when followed by <r>

marrow	garret

- When <ar> follows <w> it is pronounced /or/ in words such as war, warn, warm, ward.   Note also quart and quarter.

<ar> sounds /ar/, one phoneme, when followed by consonant other than <r>

parsnip   garment

Three or more syllable words for Reading and Dictation

<ar> sounds /ar/, one phoneme, when followed by consonant other than <r>

tarpaulin
tar/pau/lin

carpenter
car/pen/ter

narcissus
nar/cis/sus

discarded
dis/car/ded

department
de/part/ment

pharmacy
phar/mac/y

marvellous
mar/vel/lous

<ar> sounds /a/+/r/, two phonemes, when followed by <r>

embarrass
em/bar/rass

<ar> sounds /a/+/r/, two phonemes, when followed by vowel

parallel
par/al/lel

transparent
trans/par/ent

<ar> sounds /er/, one phoneme, in the final syllable of words. Spelling tip: say word as it is spelt.

regular
reg/u/lar

particular
par/tic/u/lar

Two syllable words, no more than three phonemes per syllable for Reading and Dictation

<er> has the "mixer" sound, one phoneme

gather	gopher	hanger
lumber	lobster	oyster
panther	number	powder
quarter	whisker	bitter
ginger	spider	concert
monster	dinner	desert
river	freezer	sticker
partner	sermon	lantern
certain	charter	person
beaver	prefer	shower
saunter	observe	

<er> has the sound of two separate phonemes when followed by a vowel, N.B. See Step 5.6.

very peril merry   erupt

Two syllable words, more than 3 phonemes in at least one syllable for Reading and Dictation

<er> has the "mixer" sound, one phoneme

lobsters　　　　　　**monsters**

tricksters

<er> has the sound of two separate phonemes when followed by a vowel or by <r>, N.B. See Step 5.6.

erupts　　　　　　**errand**

Three or more syllable words for Reading and Dictation

<er> has the "mixer" sound, one phoneme

minister　　　　　　min/is/ter

recover　　　　　　re/cov/er

bitterly　　　　　　bit/ter/ly

deliver　　　　　　de/liv/er

discover　　　　　　dis/cov/er

gardener　　　　　　gar/den/er

recorder　　　　　　re/cor/der

fingerprint	fing/er/print
exercise	ex/er/cise
embroider	em/broi/der
destroyer	des/troy/er
detergent	de/ter/gent
customer	cus/tom/er
carpenter	car/pen/ter
permanent	per/man/ent
remember	re/mem/ber
persevere	per/sev/ere
tuberculosis	tu/ber/cu/lo/sis
supermarket	su/per/mar/ket

operate   op/er/ate

pottery   pot/ter/y

tolerant   tol/er/ant

generous   gen/er/ous

feverish   fe/ver/ish

trickery   trick/er/y

experiment   ex/per/im/ent

different   dif/fer/ent

interrupt   in/ter/rupt

Two syllable words, no more than three phonemes per syllable for Reading and Dictation

<ir> is an alternative spelling of the /er/ sound, one phoneme, usually when followed by consonant other than <r>

dirty   skirmish

thirteen   thirsty   birthday

circus   circle

thirty   squirming

chirping   firstly   birdseed

shirking

Two syllable words, more than 3 phonemes in at least one syllable for Reading and Dictation

<ir> is an alternative spelling of the /er/ sound, one phoneme

girlfriend

<ir> sounds /i/+/r/, two phonemes, when followed by <r>

stirrup   stirring

Three or more syllable words for
Reading and Dictation

<ir> is an alternative spelling of the /er/ sound, one phoneme

circumnavigate
cir/cum/nav/ig/ate

firmament
fir/mam/ent

dirtiest
dir/ti/est (<i> in /ti/ has short sound)

<ir> sounds /i/+/r/, two phonemes, when followed by a vowel in words such as :

Miranda
Mir/an/da (final <a> is short)

miracle
mir/a/cle   (<a> is short)

<ir> sounds /i/+/r/, two phonemes, when followed by <r> in words such as:

irregular
ir/reg/u/lar

irresponsible
ir/res/pon/si/ble (<i> has short sound)

<or>

Two syllable words, no more than three phonemes per syllable for Reading and Dictation

<or> sounds /or/, one phoneme, usually when followed by consonant other than <r>

forbid	**forceful**	
forceps	**forgive**	**morning**
corner	**border**	**fortune**
hornet	**order**	**organ**
tortoise	**scorned**	**northern**
forlorn	**abhor**	**Norway**

<or> has two separate phoneme sounds /oa/+/r/ when followed by a vowel (See Step 5.6) in words such as:

glory **porous**

<or> has two separate phoneme sounds (see Step 5.6) when followed by <r>.

borrow horrid sorry corrode

<or> is a swallowed sound, pronounced as /er/, one phoneme, in the final syllable of words. Spelling tip: say word as it is spelt.

doctor **author**

- N.B. When <or> follows <w> it is pronounced /er/ in words such as work, word, worm, world, worth, worse, worst, worship.

Two syllable words, more than 3 phonemes in at least one syllable for Reading and Dictation

<or> sounds /or/, one phoneme, usually when followed by consonant other than <r>

portrait

<or> has two phoneme sounds when followed by <r>

torrent

<or> sounds /or/, one phoneme, usually when followed by consonant other than <r>

forbidden	for/bid/den
forgetful	for/get/ful
forgotten	for/got/ten
tornado	tor/na/do
torpedo	tor/pe/do
enormous	e/nor/mous or en/or/mous
subordinate	sub/or/din/ate
uniform	u/nif/orm
uniformity	u/nif/or/mit/y
discordant	dis/cor/dant
orthodox	or/thod/ox
corpulent	cor/pu/lent
forgery	for/ger/y

<or> sounds /o/+/r/, two phonemes, (see Step 5.6) when followed by a vowel in words such as :

horizon hor/i/zon

rigorous rig/or/ous

sartorial sar/tor/i/al   (<i> represents /i/)

perforate per/for/ate

corporal cor/por/al

theory the/or/y

incorporate in/cor/por/ate

explorative ex/plor/at/ive   (<ve> is alt. sp of /v/)

<or> sounds /o/+/r/, two phonemes, (see Step 5.6), when followed by <r>:

horrify hor/rif/y

horrific hor/rif/ic

incorrigible in/cor/rig/i/ble ((final <i> = /i/ sound)

corroborate cor/rob/or/ate

<or> is pronounced as /er/, one phoneme, in the final syllable of words. Spelling tip: say word as it is spelt.

aviator av/i/a/tor (short /i/ sound)

superior su/pe/ri/or (short /i/ sound)

propellor pro/pel/lor

governor gov/er/nor

> Two syllable words, no more than three phonemes per syllable for Reading and Dictation

<ur> is an alternative spelling of the /er/ sound- the "mixer" sound, one phoneme

hurting	turnip	murder
surface	furnish	further
turtle	turbine	burden
turkey	absurd	murmur
curtain	urge	survive
hurdle	furnace	curtly
sulphur	burning	
surfboard		

N.B. <oar> is alternative spelling of /or/ sound in "surfboard";
    <ace> is pronounced /us/ in "surface" and "furnace"

<ur> sounds /u/+/r/, two phonemes, when followed by <r>:

hurry	furry
Surrey	burrow

<ur> is an alternative spelling of the /er/ sound- the "mixer" sound, one phoneme

surplus **surprise** **urgent**

<ur> sounds /u/+/r/, two phonemes when followed by <r>:

flurry

<ur> is an alternative spelling of the /er/ sound- the "mixer" sound, one phoneme

turpentine   tur/pen/tine

murdering   mur/der/ing

surgery   sur/ger/y

<ur> sounds /u/+/r/, two phonemes, when followed by <r>:

hurricane   hur/ric/ane

surrender   sur/ren/der

surroundings   sur/roun/dings

Step 6.6   Sentences with r-Combination Syllable Words for Reading and Dictation

For more examples of sentences with r-combination compound words for Reading and Dictation see *Sound Discovery™ Words and Sentences Steps 1 to 3*, Step 2.3, and Step 3A.8.

<ar>

> ## Two syllable words, no more than three phonemes per syllable for Reading and Dictation

<ar> sounds /ar/, one phoneme, when followed by consonant other than <r>

1. The chickens were in the farmyard.
2. Parting is sad.
3. Can you hit the target?
4. We found fresh food in the market.
5. They grew flowers in the garden.
6. It is a wool carpet.
7. The horse had a new harness.
8. She had a scarlet dress.
9. Diamonds are a form of carbon.
10. The marble statue was in the museum.
11. The garbage went in the dustbin.
12. The chef added a lot of garlic to his cooking.
13. We were invited to a party.
14. The army went to the camp for training.
15. The loud noise may startle you.
16. His letter of thanks was tardy.

<ar> sounds /er/, one phoneme, in the final syllable of words. Spelling tip:say word as it is spelt

1. Do you like mustard with ham?
2. The sheep lost their way in the blizzard.

3.   My shirt collar is too tight.

4.   The beggar was lame and blind.

5.   Ten pillars held up the roof.

<ar> sounds /a/+/r/, two phonemes, when followed by <r>

1.   He got a prize for the biggest marrow.

2.   The artist lived in a garret.

Two syllable words, more than 3 phonemes in at least one syllable for Reading and Dictation

---

<ar> sounds /ar/, one phoneme, when followed by consonant other than <r>

1.   I love roast parsnip.

2.   Put on this garment.

Three or more syllable words for Reading and Dictation

<ar> sounds /ar/, one phoneme, when followed by consonant other than <r>

1.   Spread the tarpaulin on the floor of the tent.

2.   The carpenter mended the door.

3.   She had a bunch of white narcissus.

4.   We discarded the broken cups.

5.   The maths department is large.

6.   She got the drugs from the pharmacy.

7.   There was a marvellous sunset.

<ar> sounds /a/+/r/, two phonemes, when followed by <r>

1.   I do not want to embarrass you.

<ar> sounds /a/+/r/, two phonemes, when followed by a vowel

1.   Parallel lines do not cross.

2.   The fabric is transparent.

<ar> sounds /er/, one phoneme, in the final syllable of words. Spelling tip: say word as it is spelt.

1.   My regular drink is diet coke.

2.   I am particular about my friends.

Two syllable words, no more than three phonemes per syllable for Reading and Dictation

<er> has the "mixer" sound, one phoneme

1. Can you gather up the toys?
2. A gopher is a rodent.
3. The plane was kept in the hanger.
4. They put the trunk in the lumber room.
5. He ate a bad oyster.
6. A black panther killed the goat.
7. I live at number six.
8. She patted her face with powder.
9. We can have a quarter of the apple each.
10. The car missed the child by a whisker.
11. The drink is bitter.
12. He added ginger to the stir fry.
13. The spider spun a big web.
14. They went out to a concert.
15. The story was about a monster.
16. We have dinner at eight o'clock.
17. The camel train went across the desert.
18. The river has good trout.
19. You will find some ice in the freezer.
20. Gavin got a sticker for good work.
21. You need a partner for the dance.
22. The vicar preached a long sermon.

23.   He held up a lantern to light my path.

24.   I am certain he will be here soon.

25.   The town kept its royal charter in the safe.

26.   The gun was hidden on his person.

27.   The beaver constructed a dam.

28.   I prefer my eggs soft boiled.

29.   He takes his shower at night.

30.   Young men like to saunter down the road.

31.   A teacher needs to observe her pupils.

<er> has the sound of two separate phonemes when followed by a vowel, N.B. Step 5.6

1.   The old man is very sick.

2.   Take out the boat at your peril.

3.   Robin Hood sat down with his merry men.

4.   The volcano began to erupt.

<er> has the "mixer" sound, one phoneme

1.   We had lobsters for supper.

2.   The children were little monsters.

3.   A trickster is a person who plays tricks.

<er> has the sound of two separate phonemes when followed by a vowel or by <r>, N.B. See Step 5.6

1.   Trouble erupts on the march.

2.   His mum sent him on an errand.

<er> has the "mixer" sound, one phoneme

1.   The church has a good minister.

2.   He will recover when he goes home.

3.   The victim cried bitterly.

4.   Deliver us from evil!

5.   You will not discover her secret

6.   The gardener planted the bulbs.

7.   She plays the recorder in the band.

8.   You can see a fingerprint on the glass.

9.   We need to take more exercise.

10.   The dress maker will embroider the veil.

11.   We saw the navy destroyer at sea.

12.   You will need detergent to clean the clothes.

13.   The customer is always right.

14.   The carpenter mended the broken table.

15.   She is a permanent member of the team.

16.   Remember what happened yesterday.

17.   If you persevere you will succeed.

18.   The poet died from tuberculosis.

19.   We did the shopping in the supermarket.

<er> has the sound of two separate phonemes when followed by a vowel or by <r>, N.B. See Step 5.6

1.   When will they operate on the baby?

2.   She makes pottery.

3.   The mother duck is tolerant of her chicks.

4.   The rich man gave a generous gift.

5.   The sick child was feverish.

6.   I was taken in by his trickery.

7.   The chemistry experiment was successful.

8.   Can you do something different?

9.   Please do not interrupt me.

<ir>

<ir> is an alternative spelling of the /er/ sound, one phoneme

1. His trousers were dirty.
2. The bandits had a skirmish in the desert.
3. My son is thirteen years old today.
4. Gardening makes you thirsty.
5. Are you having a birthday party?
6. The circus came to town.
7. Draw a circle on the paper!
8. There are thirty pupils in the class.
9. The snakes were squirming in the snake pit.
10. The chicks are chirping for more food.
11. Firstly you set the table.
12. Can you put birdseed in the cage?
13. My boss will not tolerate any shirking.

Two syllable words, more than 3 phonemes in at least one syllable for Reading and Dictation

<ir> is an alternative spelling of the /er/ sound

1. He has a new girlfriend.

<ir> sounds /i/+/r/, two phonemes, when followed by <r>

1. You need to tighten the stirrup.
2. Keep stirring the pot with the wooden spoon!

Three or more syllable words for Reading and Dictation

<ir> is an alternative spelling of the /er/ sound

1. The explorer will circumnavigate the globe.
2. The stars shine brightly in the firmament.
3. He is the dirtiest puppy in the litter.

<ir> sounds /i/+/r/, two phonemes, when followed by <r>

1. Miranda came to stay.
2. His recovery was a miracle.

<ir> sounds /i/+/r/, two phonemes, when follwed by <r>

1. We need to learn these irregular verbs.
2. It was an irresponsible thing to do.

> Two syllable words, no more than three phonemes per syllable for Reading and Dictation

<or> sounds /or/, one phoneme, usually when followed by consonant other than <r>

1. I forbid you to talk of it.
2. He has a forceful personality.
3. The baby had a forceps delivery.
4. Father forgive them!
5. We take tea in the morning.
6. You will find the shop round the corner.
7. We stopped at the Scottish border.
8. The gypsy told his fortune.
9. A hornet is an insect with a severe sting.
10. We need to order more supplies.
11. The church had a new organ.
12. The tortoise has a strong shell.
13. She was scorned by her lover.
14. We saw the Northerns Lights in the sky.
15. The maiden looked forlorn.
16. I abhor lies.
17. The boat sailed to Norway.

<or. has two separate sounds /oa/+/r/ when followed by a vowel

1. They gazed at the glory of the sunset.
2. An unglazed pot is porous.

1. Can I borrow some money?

2. The drink tastes horrid.

3. He is sorry you are upset.

4. Acid will corrode the metal.

<or> has a swallowed sound, pronounced as /er/, one phoneme, in the final syllable of words. Stelling tip: say word as it is spelt

1. The doctor will make me better.

2. He is the author of the book.

Two syllable words, more than 3 phonemes in at least one syllable for Reading and Dictation

<or> sounds /or/, one phoneme, usually when followed by consonant other than <r>

1. The artist painted her portrait.

<or> has two phoneme sounds when followed by <r>

1. The heavy rains made the river a torrent.

Three or more syllable words, for Reading and Dictation

<or> sounds /or/, one phoneme, usually when followed by consonant other than <r>

1. It is forbidden to walk on the grass.

2. The old man is getting forgetful.

3. A tornado destroyed the town.

4. A torpedo sank the ship.

5. He has an enormous house.

6. A subordinate should obey orders.

7. The waitress put on her uniform.

8. The army likes uniformity.

9.   The trumpet made a discordant noise.

10.   He is an orthodox Jew.

11.   The corpulant man could not fit into the seat.

12.   This bank note is a forgery.

<or> sounds /o/+/r/, two phonemes, when followed by a v owel

1.   The sun sank below the horizon.

2.   She gave her car a rigorous clean.

3.   His tailor sees to his sartorial needs.

4.   You need to perforate the bag with a knife.

5.   He was promoted to corporal.

6.   Have you passed your theory test?

7.   We should incorporate him into the team.

8.   They made an explorative trip into the forest.

<or> sounds /o/+/r/, two phonemes, when followed by <r>

1.   The sight of his scar will horrify you.

2.   She sustained horrific cuts to her legs.

3.   The black sheep of the family is incorrigible.

4.   The witness will corroborate my story.

<or> is pronounced as /er/, one phoneme, in the final syllable of words. Spelling tip: say word as it is spelt.

1.   The aviator flew the plane.

2.   My superior is a just person.

3.   The old plane had a wooden propellor.

4.   The governor of the prison left.

<ur>

<table><tr><td>Two syllable words, no more than three phonemes per syllable for Reading and Dictation</td></tr></table>

<ur> is an alternative spelling of the /er/ sound - the "mixer" sound, one phoneme

1. Is your leg hurting?
2. They had turnip and greens with the meat.
3. He spoke of a dreadful murder.
4. The surface of the lake was smooth.
5. We need to furnish the room with new items.
6. The turtle laid her eggs in the sand.
7. A turbine is a type of machine.
8. The donkey is called a beast of burden.
9. We had a turkey for dinner.
10. He told an absurd story.
11. She agreed without a murmur of protest.
12. I am certain he will come.
13. We urge you to reconsider.
14. How can you survive with so little food?
15. The first hurdle is to pass your test.
16. They burnt the rubbish in the furnace.
17. The teacher spoke curtly to the pupil.
18. Sulphur is yellow.
19. The wood is burning on the bonfire.
20. He took his surfboard to the beach.

1.   Hurry up or you will be late!

2.   The kitten is soft and furry.

3.   We now live in Surrey.

4.   The rabbit ran down its burrow.

Two syllable words, more than 3 phonemes in at least one syllable for Reading and Dictation

<ur> is an alternative spelling of the /er/ sound - the "mixer" sound, one phoneme

1.   Let us sell off the surplus apples.

2.   His arrival was a surprise.

3.   My meeting is urgent.

<ur> sounds /u/+/r/, two phonemes, when followed by <r>

1.   A flurry of snow covered the grass.

Three or more syllable words, for Reading and Dictation

<ur> is an alternative spelling of the /er/ sound - the "mixer" sound, one phoneme

1.   Turpentine is a good solvent for paint.

2   You are murdering that song.

3.   She needs surgery on her leg.

<ur> sounds /u/+/r/, two phonemes, when followed by <r>

1.   The house was damaged in the hurricane.

2.   He ordered the man to surrender his gun.

3.   Are you happy in your surroundings?

STEP 7   TEACH SPECIAL SUFFIXES

Some polysyllabic words contain special suffixes which can be considered as individual chunks or units.

Special suffixes can be taught using the flash card materials found in the *Sound Discovery*™ *Manual*, pages 93-96.

The special suffixes can be taught through the *Snappy Lesson*™.

Each special suffix has a special sound. These sounds can be represented by a sound picture; for example <tion> is a sound picture of the sound /shun/.

Students can practise with polysyllabic words containing the special suffixes and sentences containing these words. Students should practise reading the suffixes, words and sentences and also spelling them from dictation.

Teach Special Suffixes using the *Snappy Lesson*™

INTRODUCTION

- Teacher shows the suffix card <tion> photocopied from the *Sound Discovery*™ *Manual*, page 93.
- Teacher says, "This is /shun/. It sounds like it should be spelled like this": <shun>.
- Teacher writes the letters on the board saying each phoneme as he/she writes it:

sh u n. Teacher says, "/shun/ is a special suffix which comes at the ends of words which we can remember like a picture." Teacher shows the suffix card <tion> and says, " This is one picture of /shun/."

- Students say /shun/ whilst looking at suffix card <tion>.
- Teacher then shows the suffix card <sion> photocopied from the *Sound Discovery Manual*, page 93.
- Teacher says, "This is another picture of /shun/ These are two alternative spellings of /shun/."
- Students say /shun/ in response to both suffix cards.

 (It may be of interest to reflect that <tion> splits into graphemes ti-o-n and that these letters represent the phonemes sh-u-n. <o> is an alternative spelling of the /u/ sound as in "son". <sion> splits si-o-n and these graphemes also represent the phonemes sh-u-n. <si> is another way to spell the /sh/ sound.)

The teacher can then follow the *Snappy Lesson*™ using the special suffixes, words and sentences in Step 7.

READING

---

1. SPECIAL SUFFIXES   quick review of any special suffixes already taught

- Teacher shows the suffix cards photocopied from the *Sound Discovery*™ *Manual* pp 93-96.
- Student says whole suffix.

---

2. SPECIAL SUFFIXES   teach new suffix

- Teacher uses suffix card from *Sound Discovery*™ *Manual* e.g. -tion.
- Students say whole suffix.

---

3. BLENDING   oral blending

- Teacher says whole syllable(s) and special suffix using "robot arms" if necessary,   e.g.sta-tion, vac-a-tion.
- Students blend the separate chunks into the word.

---

4. WORD CARDS   (from Step 7, *Sound Discovery*™ *Words and Sentences, Part 2*)
sound and say

- Students sound syllables and special suffix chunk, using "robot arms" if necessary, they blend the chunks together and say the word.
- Students sound in their heads and say word.

---

5. WORD LISTS

- Whole group reads lists from *Sound Discovery*™ *Words and Sentences, Part2*.
- Teacher asks individual students to read specific words.

---

6. SENTENCE READING

- Use *Sound Discovery*™ *Words and Sentences, Part 2* and controlled texts.

SPELLING

---

1. SPECIAL SUFFIXES   **quick review of any special suffixes already taught**

- Teacher dictates special suffix chunks.
- Students say each chunk slowly as they write the chunk on small white board. Do not allow them to say letter names as they write the special suffix.

---

2. SPECIAL SUFFIXES   **teach new spelling pattern**

- Teacher explains, "This is the new picture of the special ending/suffix for today."
- Teacher says the special ending and shows the new spelling on a card photocopied from the *Sound Discovery*™ *Manual* pp. 93-96.
- Teacher models letter formation, saying the chunk slowly as he/she writes it. Teacher does not say letter names.
- Teacher says special suffix to the students.
- Students repeat chunk slowly as they write the suffix. They do not say letter names.

---

3. HEARING THE SYLLABLES AND SPECIAL SUFFIXES IN WORDS

- Teacher says word to group, e.g. station.
- Students repeat the word, saying it slowly to identify the syllable(s) and special suffix, by clapping beats or feeling the lowering of the chin.
- Students say syllable, count phonemes of the syllable on fingers of one hand and show fingers.
- Students say whole suffix and identify it with closed fist of other hand, e.g. s-t-a-/tion.
- Teacher says word to individual student, e.g. vacation.
- Student says syllables and special suffix: vac/a/tion. Student repeats first syllable, identifying phonemes on fingers of one hand, and makes the syllable on board with magnetic phoneme cards from *Sound Discovery*™ *Manual*: v-a-c. Student repeats with other syllable(s):a. Student repeats special suffix and places magnetic suffix card <tion> from *Sound Discovery*™ *Manual* to the right of vac and a.
- Student says word.

---

4. SPELLING

- Teacher dictates word from Step 7, e.g. election.
- Students identify syllables and special suffix: e/lec/tion.
- Students tap phoneme(s) for first syllable on white board.
- Students draw phoneme line(s) for first syllable on white board: _
- Students write in letter(s) and say syllable: <u>e</u>
- Leave a space
- Tap, draw phoneme lines and write in letters for second and subsequent syllables:
<u>e</u>   <u>l e c</u>
- Leave a space.
- Draw a special suffix line and write letters in whilst saying the chunk: <u>tion</u>
- Student says word: <u>e</u>   <u>l e c</u>   <u>tion</u>
- Teacher models correct response on board.

---

5. SENTENCES

- Teacher dictates sentences using new spelling pattern from controlled text or from Step 7, *Sound Discovery*™ *Words and Sentences, Part 2.*
- Students write sentence and read it back.
- Teacher models correct response on board.

- Incorporate into independent writing through modelling.

Step 7.1 Words with Alternative Spellings
for Special Suffix /shun/
for Reading and Dictation
tion sion ssion cion cian cean

Words with the <ti>, <si> and <ci> spellings are from a Latin background, with one exception, the <cian> words. The accent is always on the vowel which predeces the special suffix. When <a>,<o>,<u> come directly before the suffix they are always long. When <i > comes before the suffix it is always short.

<tion>
<a> before suffix

vacation	nation
explanation	plantation
indignation	taxation
coronation	pagination
flirtation station	relation
education	operation
multiplication	accusation
celebration	population
accommodation location	

association **conversation**

hesitation **investigation**

situation

vac/a/tion, na/tion, ex/plan/a/tion, plan/ta/tion, in/dig/na/tion, tax/a/tion, cor/on/a/tion, pag/in/a/tion, flir/ta/tion, sta/tion, re/la/tion, ed/uc/a/tion, op/er/a/tion, mul/tip/lic/a/tion, ac/cu/sa/tion, cel/eb/ra/tion, pop/u/la/tion, ac/com/mod/a/tion, as/soc/i/a/tion, loc/a/tion, con/ver/sa/tion, hes/it/a/tion, in/ves/tig/a/tion, sit/u/a/tion

<o> before suffix

motion **potion**

emotion **commotion**

locomotion **devotion**

mo/tion, po/tion, e/mo/tion, com/mo/tion, lo/co/mo/tion, de/vo/tion

<u> before suffix

revolution **resolution**

constitution

rev/o/lu/tion, res/o/lu/tion, con/stit/u/tion

<i > before suffix

condition ignition ambition

tuition sedition addition

expedition disposition

preposition   proposition

opposition   composition

con/di/tion, ig/ni/tion, am/bi/tion, tu/i/tion, sed/i/tion, ad/di/tion, ex/ped/i/tion, dis/pos/i/tion, prep/os/i/tion, prop/os/t/tion, op/pos/i/tion, com/pos/i/tion

vowel digraph or consonant before suffix

caution   action   affection

objection   mention   fiction

description   precaution

direction   instruction

intention   caption attention

subtraction   infection

election   connection

collection

cau/tion, ac/tion, af/fec/tion, ob/jec/tion, men/tion, fic/tion, des/crip/tion, pre/cau/tion, di/rec/tion, in/struc/tion, in/ten/tion, cap/tion, at/ten/tion, sub/trac/tion, in/fec/tion, e/lec/tion, con/nec/tion, col/lec/tion

<sion>

When a vowel is directly before <sion> the special suffix usually sounds /zhun/, as in vision. When <sion> has a consonant before it, <sion> usually sounds /shun/, as in extension. The following section deals only with the /shun/ sound of the special suffix <sion>.

consonant before suffix

extension   **comprehension**

ascension

convulsion   **propulsion**

expulsion   **dimension**

suspension   **expansion**

compulsion   **apprehension**

version   **immersion**

perversion   **excursion**

ex/ten/sion, com/pre/hen/sion, as/cen/sion, de/scen/sion, con/vul/sion, pro/pul/sion, ex/pul/sion, di/men/sion, sus/pen/sion, ex/pan/sion, com/pul/sion, appre/hen/sion, ver/sion, im/mer/sion, per/ver/sion, ex/cur/sion.

<ssion>

As with -tion, and -sion, such words are from a Latin background. The accent is always on the vowel which predeces the special suffix. The vowel before the special suffix is usually short. Another way of looking at the split is the first <s> of the special suffix belonging to the previous syllable, making it a closed syllable, thus ensuring the vowel sound is short, e.g. pas/sion. However, this present analysis will make use of the special suffix -ssion split.

passion

<a>before suffix

pa/ssion

discussion

<u> before suffix

dis/cu/ssion
<i > before suffix

mission	**commission**
admission	**permission**

mi/ssion, com/mi/sion, ad/mi/ssion, per/mi/ssion
<e> before suffix

expression	**congressional**
depression	**impression**
concession	**succession**
oppression	**impression**
recession	**repression**
profession	**confession**
transgression	**progression**

ex/pre/ssion, con/gre/ssion/al, de/pre/ssion, im/pre/ssion, con/ce/ssion, suc/ce/ssion, op/pre/ssion, im/pre/ssion, re/ce/ssion, re/pre/ssion, pro/fe/ssion, con/fe/ssion, trans/gre/ssion, pro/gre/ssion

<cion>

coercion

suspicion

co/er/cion, sus/pi/cion

<cian>

This group of /shun/ words is from Greek. The stem of the word is Greek and it always ends in <c>, followed by the connective <i> forming the /sh/ sound. The remainder of the special suffix is <-an> (but not <-on>), and means "a person who". The special suffix is <cian> and it sounds /shun/.

musician   physician

magician   electrician

politician   mathematician

mu/si/cian, phys/i/cian, mag/i/cian, el/ec/tri/cian, pol/it/i/cian, math/em/at/i/cian

<cean>

ocean

o/cean

Step 7.1 Sentences with Alternative Spellings for Special Suffix /shun/ for Reading and Dictation

tion   sion   ssion   cion   cian   cean

<tion>

<a> before suffix

1. We went on vacation to the seaside.
2. The President gave his Address to the Nation.
3. You need to give me an explanation.
4. The plantation grew cotton.
5, She snorted in indignation.
6. Taxation can be a big burden.
7. We had a holiday on the Queen's coronation.
8. The computer can help with pagination.
9. She cannot resist a little flirtation.
10. I can meet you at the station.
11. He is a long lost relation of mine.
12. The children got a good education.
13. He went to hospital for an operation.
14. She has difficulty with multiplication.
15. He denied the accusation.
16. This calls for a celebration.
17. The population has grown.
18. I need some comfortable accommodation.

19.   The film was shot on location in Spain.

20.   I belong to the association.

21.   We had a good conversation.

22.   You must speak without hesitation.

23.   The investigation was painful.

24.   Does the situation trouble you?

<o> before suffix

1.   The motion of the train makes me sick.

2.   Take this potion twice a day.

3.   He was overcome with emotion.

4.   Did you see the commotion in the street?

5.   The streamlined shape helps locomotion.

6.   His followers showed their devotion.

<u> before suffix

1.   The wheel made a complete revolution.

2.   The committee passed a resolution.

3.   The United States has a constitution

<i > before suffix

1.   The race horse is in peak condition.

2.   Turn on the ignition!

3.   His ambition is to be a pilot.

4.   He had tuition on the violin.

5.   He was jailed for sedition.

6.   The baby is a new addition to the family.

7.	The men set out on an expedition.

8.	The dog has a gentle disposition.

9.	Can you find a preposition in the sentence?

10.	They voted on the proposition.

11.	He is in opposition to your idea.

12.	She played his new composition.

vowel digraph or consonant before suffix

1.	Cross the road with caution.

2.	He is a man of action.

3.	She regards her pupil with affection.

4.	I have no objection to the plan.

5.	You must mention this to Dad.

6.	His story is a fiction.

7.	The man fitted my description.

8.	You should take every precaution.

9.	Can you point me in the right direction?

10.	The learner needs more instruction.

11.	I have no intention of failing.

12.	The caption under the cartoon was funny.

13.	Stand to attention!

14.	This problem involves subtraction.

15.	She has a chest infection.

16.	My party won the election.

17.	What is the connection between the two?

18.	He has a collection of fine china.

<sion>

consonant before suffix

1. The extension to the house is finished.

2. I find reading comprehension hard.

3. Ascension Day is in the church calendar.

4. The feverish child had a convulsion.

5. Flippers give a swimmer good propulsion.

6. We regret the boy's expulsion from school.

7. He added a new dimension to politics.

8. The girl had a three day suspension from school.

9. This gap allows for thermal expansion.

10. There is no compulsion about joining.

11. I feel some apprehension about going.

12. The second version of the song is shorter.

13. An immersion heater is expensive to run.

14. His story is a perversion of the truth.

15. They went on a coach excursion to Scotland.

<ssion>

<a> before suffix

1.   He burst into a passion of sobs.

<u> before suffix

1.   The discussion became heated.

<i> before suffix

1.   He has a mission to save the whale.
2.   She takes a commission on every purchase.
3.   The admission charge is five pounds.
4.   Can I have permission to go out?

<e> before suffix

1.   Her face had a joyful expression.
2.   They attended a congressional meeting.
3.   Dad sank into a black depression.
4.   I got the impression you were unhappy.
5.   There is a concession for the elderly.
6.   We had a succession of visitors.
7.   Their oppression by the Romans was cruel.
8.   What impression did you form of the play?
9.   The banks were badly hit by the recession.
10.   She could not tolerate his repression any more.
11.   Teaching is a noble profession.
12.   I have a confession to make.
13.   Her transgression was forgiven.
14.   He had a progression of girlfriends.

<cion>

<r> or <i > before suffix

1.   The prisoner needed some coercion.

2.   He is held on suspicion of the crime.

<cian>

<i > before suffix

1.   The musician played his violin.

2.   The physician healed me.

3.   The magician pulled a rabbit out of the hat.

4.   The electrician fitted the new light.

5.   The politician lost his seat at the election.

6.   The mathematician solved the problem.

<cean>

1.   We sailed across the Atlantic Ocean.

Step 7.2 Words with Special Suffix /kshun/ for Reading and Dictation xion

The sound of <x> is /k/+/s/, hence <xion> sounds /kshun/. The words are of Latin background and the accent is on the vowel which precedes <xion>. When <a>, <o> or <u> come directly before the suffix they are always long. When <i > comes before the suffix it is always short. When <e> comes before the suffix, both long and short vowel sounds must be tried.

<xion>

crucifixion   complexion

cru/cif/i/xion, com/ple/xion

Step 7.2 Sentences with Special Suffix /kshun/ for Reading and Dictation xion

<xion>

1. The painting depicted the Crucifixion of Christ.

2. She has a peaches and cream complexion.

Step 7.3 Words with Special Suffix /zhun/ for Reading and Dictation
sion

<sion> sometimes sounds /zhun/, usually when it comes directly after a vowel. When it has a consonant before it, <sion> usually sounds /shun/, as in extension. These words are also from a Latin background. The accent is always on the vowel which predeces the special suffix. When <a>,<o>,<u> come directly before the suffix these vowels are always long. When <i > comes before the suffix it is always short.

<a> before suffix

invasion

abrasion

occasion

persuasion

in/va/sion, ab/ra/sion, oc/ca/sion, per/sua/sion

<o> before suffix

explosion

erosion

ex/plo/sion, er/o/sion

fusion

confusion

transfusion

profusion

inclusion

exclusion

collusion

fu/sion, con/fu/sion, trans/fu/sion, pro/fu/sion, in/clu/sion, ex/clu/sion, col/lu/sion

vision

television

supervision

precision

decision

division

indecision

provision

revision

derision

vi/sion, tel/e/vi/sion, sup/er/vi/sion, pre/ci/sion, de/ci/sion, div/i/sion, in/de/ci/sion, pro/vi/sion, re/vi/sion, de/ri/sion

Step 7.3   Sentences with Special Suffix /zhun/ for Reading and Dictation

<sion>

<a> before suffix

1.	The invasion came from the East.
2.	He suffered an abrasion on his heel.
3.	On this occasion I will forgive you.
4.	She needed no persuasion to come.

<o> before suffix

1.	The explosion killed three men.
2.	The cliffs show some erosion.

<u> before suffix

1.	This music is a fusion of jazz and funk.
2.	There was some confusion about times.
3.	Bob had to have a blood transfusion.
4.	We saw a profusion of bluebells in the wood.
5.	She insisted on the inclusion of all children.
6.	The exclusion of girls is not right.
7.	I suspect collusion between the two witnesses.

<i > before suffix

1.	The new glasses improve his vision.
2.	I saw the film on television.
3.	He was given a supervision order.
4.	This is a precision instrument.
5.	Her friends helped her to make the decision.
6.	Can you do division in your head.
7.	He was gripped with indecision.
8.	Her extra provision was five hours teaching.
9.	I need to do some revision for my exam.
10.	The prophet was an object of derision.

Step 7.4 Words with AlternativeSpellings for Special Suffix /shus/ for Reading and Dictation
cious   tious scious

These words are also from a Latin background. The accent is always on the vowel which predeces the special suffix. When <a>,<o>,<u> come directly before the suffix these vowels are always long. When <i > comes before the suffix it is always short. <e> is less frequently found and must be tried both ways.

<cious>

<a> before suffix

voracious   **spacious**

gracious   **fallacious**

vor/a/cious, spa/cious, gra/cious, fal/la/cious

<o> before suffix

precocious   **atrocious**

ferocious

pre/co/cious, at/ro/cious, fer/o/cious

<i > before suffix

delicious   **vicious**

malicious   **avaricious**

auspicious

del/i/cious, vi/cious, mat/ri/cious, av/ar/i/cious, aus/pi/cious

precious

pre/cious

<tious>

ambitious

fictitious

nutritious

am/bi/tious, fic/ti/tious, nu/tri/cious

facetious

fac/e/tious (<c> followed by <e> has /s/ sound)

infectious

in/fec/tious

<scious>

conscious

con/scious

Step 7.4 Sentences with Alternative Spellings for Special Suffix /shus/ for Reading and Dictation

cious   tious   scious

<cious>

<a> before suffix

1. Teenagers have voracious appetites.

2. The new house has spacious rooms.

3. The Queen was very gracious.

4. The story is fallacious.

<o> before suffix

1. The child showed precocious development.

2. We had atrocious weather on holiday.

3. The tiger gave a ferocious snarl.

<i> before suffix

1. We ate a delicious meal.

2. The vicious dog attacked the postman.

3. How did the malicious story start?

4. The avaricious man craved more wealth.

5. The black cat was seen as an auspicious sign.

6. Precious stones were found in the mine.

<tious>

<i> before suffix

1. The new library is an ambitious project.

2. The characters in the book are all fictitious.

3. The meal was nutritious.

<e> before suffix

1. His facetious remark was not welcomed.

consonant before suffix

1. Smallpox is infectious.

<scious>

1. He was fully conscious during his operation.

Step 7.5 Words with Special Suffix /kshus/ for Reading and Dictation
xious

The sound of <x> is /k/+/s/, hence <xious> sounds /kshus/

<xious>

obnoxious   anxious

ob/no/xious: This can be viewed as ob/nok/cious with the <o> as short.

an/xious: This can be viewed as ank/cious. <nk> in words like "ink" is pronounced as /ng+k/ with the <g> omitted in the spelling but not in the sound. Similarly, "anxious" sounds: a-ng-k-sh-u-s. In the spelling, <g> is omitted, the sounds /k/+/s/ are represented by the letter <x> and the letters <xi> represent the sounds /k+sh/.   "ink" should really be spelt as ingk and "anxious" should really be spelt angxious.

Step 7.5 Sentences with Special Suffix /kshus/ for Reading and Dictation
xious

<xious>

1. The obnoxious man was disliked by all.

2. Waiting for exam results is an anxious time.

Step 7.6 Words with Special Suffix /shu/ for Reading and Dictation

tia   cia

<tia>

militia   inertia   dementia

mil/i/tia, in/er/tia, de/men/tia

<cia>

facia   Patricia   Marcia

fa/cia, Pat/ri/cia, Mar/cia

Step 7.6 Sentences with Special Suffix /shu/ for Reading and Dictation

tia   cia

<tia>

1. A militia is composed of citizens.
2. The sleepy girl was overcome by inertia.
3. The old man suffered from dementia.

<cia>

1. The facia boards on our house need painting.
2. My best friend is Patricia.
3. Marcia came to visit us yesterday.

Step 7.7 Words with Special Suffix /zhu/ for Reading and Dictation
sia

<sia>

Asia   Malaysia

amnesia   freesia   Persia

A/sia, Mal/a/sia, am/ne/sia, free/sia, Per/sia

Step 7.7 Sentences with Special Suffix /zhu/ for Reading and Dictation
sia

<sia>

1. Asia is the largest continent.

2. Malasia is in the Commonwealth.

3. After he hit his head he suffered from amnesia.

4. The freesia has fragrant flowers.

5. Persia is the former name of Iran.

Step 7.8 Words with Special Suffix /cher/ for Reading and Dictation

ture

The accent pattern can be different in these words. In a **two syllable** word the accent is usually on the syllable which predeces the special suffix.   The vowels <a>,<o>,<u> in accented syllables which come directly before the special suffix are always long (e.g. na/ture, fu/ture). In words with **more syllables** the accent often falls on the first syllable. In these words the vowel which precedes the special ending in unaccented syllables is usually short (e.g. sig/na/ture, min/i/a/ture, lit/er/a/ture). Practically all <i>s in unaccented syllables are short (e.g. fur/ni/ture, min/i/a/ture - in everyday speech this /i/ is not usually pronounced and the word sounds: min/a/ture).

<ture>

<a> and <o> before suffix in accented syllables (these vowel sounds are long)

nature   future

consonant before suffix in two syllable words (vowels in closed syllables are short)

gesture   posture   capture

pasture   fracture   picture

lecture   structure   texture

culture   mixture

<a> and <i > before suffix in unaccented syllable in words of more than 2 syllables (vowel sounds are short)

temperature   miniature

literature   signature

furniture

consonant before suffix in words of more than 2 syllables (vowel sounds in closed syllables are short)

architecture   adventure

na/ture, fu/ture, ges/ture, pos/ture, cap/ture, pas/ture, frac/ture, pic/ture, lec/ture, struc/ture, tex/ture, cul/ture, mix/ture, tem/per/a/ture, min/i/a/ture, lit/er/a/ture, sig/na/ture, ar/chi/tec/ture, ad/ven/ture

Step 7.8 Sentences with Special Suffix /cher/ for Reading and Dictation
ture

<a> and <o> before suffix in accented syllables (these vowel sounds are long)

1. It is not in his nature to be bad tempered.
2. The good student has a bright future.

consonant before suffix in two syllable words (vowel in closed syllables are short)

1. In France I use a lot of gesture while speaking.
2. The officer has an erect posture.
3. You must capture the escaped lion.
4. The cows are grazing on the pasture.
5. He has a severe fracture of the femur.
6. Her face is a picture.
7. They attended the lecture.
8. His job gives a structure to his life.
9. Silk has a smooth texture.
10. It can be a culture shock to move to a big city.
11. The cook put the cake mixture into the oven.

<a> and <i > before suffix in unaccented syllable in words of more than 2 syllables (vowel sounds are short)

1. Check the temperature of your bath!
2. He found a miniature for his collection.
3. The student is studying literature.
4. Can you write your signature here?
5. I must polish the furniture.

consonant before suffix in words of more than two syllables (vowel sounds in closed syllables are short)

1. Clifton Cathedral won a prize for its architecture.
2. The Famous Five had one last adventure.

Step 7.9 Words with Special Suffix /zher/ for Reading and Dictation
sure

<o> before suffix in words of two syllables

closure

alternative spellings of /e/ sound before suffix

treasure   pleasure   leisure

measure

<o> before suffix in words of more than two syllables

exposure   composure

clo/sure, trea/sure, plea/sure, lei/sure, mea/sure, ex/po/sure, com/po/sure

Step 7.9 Sentences with Special Suffix /zher/ for Reading and Dictation
sure

<o> before suffix in words of two syllables

1. We protested about the closure of the cinema.

alternative spellings of /e/ sound before suffix

1. The children looked for hidden treasure.

2. They took pleasure in the music.

3. Read it at your leisure.

4. Measure the room for the new carpet.

<o> before suffix in words of more than two syllables

1. Your back has had too much exposure to the sun.

2. After her outburst she regained her composure.

Step 7.10 Words with Special Suffix /sher/ for Reading and Dictation

ssure

The following are two-syllable words where the accent is on the syllable which predeces the special suffix.. The vowels <e> and <i> are short.

<e> before suffix

pressure

<i > before suffix

fissure

pre/ssure, fi/ssure

Step 7.10 Sentences with Special Suffix /sher/ for Reading and Dictation

ssure

<e> before suffix

1.   The pressure of work was too much for him.

<i > before suffix

2.   A fissure is a long, narrow crack in a rock.

Step 7.11 Words with Special Suffix /shul/ for Reading and Dictation

tial   cial

<tial>

<a> before suffix in accented syllables (these vowel sounds are long)

spatial   palatial

<i> before suffix in accented syllable is short

initial

r controlled syllable before suffix is one phoneme

martial   partial

consonant before suffix (vowel in closed syllable is short)

substantial

spa/tial, pal/a/tial, in/i/tial, mar/tial, par/tial, sub/stan/tial

<cial>

<a> before suffix is long   <u> before suffix is long

spacial (alternative spelling of spatial)   crucial

<e> before suffix can be long or short (short in this example)

special

<i> before suffix is short

judicial   official

beneficial   artificial

spa/cial, spe/cial, ju/di/cial, of/fi/cial, ben/e/fi/cial, ar/ti/fi/cial

Step 7.11 Sentences with Special Suffix /shul/ for Reading and Dictation
tial   cial

<tial>

<a> before suffix is long

1.   Her spatial skills are not good.

2.   Their new house is palatial.

<i> before suffix is short

1.   The initial meeting was successful.

r controlled syllable before suffix is one phoneme

1.   The fighter studied the martial arts.

2.   There was a partial eclipse of the sun.

consonant before suffix (vowel in closed syllable is short)

1.   She left a substantial sum of money.

<cial>

<a> before suffix is long

1.   Use your spacial skills to make this jigsaw!

<u> before suffix is long

1.   The fingerprint was a crucial bit of evidence.

<e> before suffix is short in this example

1.   She is a special friend.

<i> before suffix is short

1.   A judicial review was requested.

2.   He is a member of the official fan club.

3.   An apple a day is beneficial for health.

4.   The land mine victim had an artificial leg.